Showers of Blessings

Devotional

Cecilia D. Porter

Copyright © 2023 by Cecilia D. Porter
All rights reserved

Table of Contents

- SHOWERS OF BLESSINGS 1
- "THE I WILL GOD" 5
- PROOF OF THE RESURRECTION..9
- SOMEBODY'S WATCHING YOU! 15
- 1,440 MINUTES 20
- THE GOD OF THE IMPOSSIBLE 23
- LIVING IN THE MOMENT 27
- OUR ARCH ENEMY #1 30
- THOSE THAT LOVES GOD 34
- IF ONLY 40
- SEEING GOD IN EVERYTHING 43
- SINGING THE BLUES 46
- WEEDS OF LIFE 50
- MY CROSS TO BEAR..54

- A RED SEA EXPERIENCE 57
- WHO IS WAITING ON WHO? 61
- GOD'S DIVINE PROVIDENCE 64
- GOD'S INESCAPABLE PRESENCE 67
- THIS IS ONLY A TEST! 71
- THE DELAYED PRAYER DEPARTMENT 77
- SUFFICIENT GRACE 81
- JESUS' PEACE 84
- FRUIT OF THE SPIRIT 88
- SALVATION 91
- WHY? 95
- THE HEART 99
- HARD-HEARTED 102
- WINGS TO FLY AWAY 105
- MERCY'S DOOR 109
- NEVERTHELESS 113
- POTHOLES OF LIFE 118
- "IT" 122
- UNRAVELING 126
- HERO! 130
- VILLAIN? 135
- VICTIM? 140
- ANGUISH 143
- THE DOMINO EFFECT 147
- GOOD MORNING, HEARTBREAK! 152
- MISERY LOVES COMPANY 155
- THE LORD IS MY SHEPHERD 158
- YOUR IMAGINATION 162
- RELATIONSHIPS 166

- A DAMASCUS ROAD EXPERIENCE 170
- LOVE! 174
- WHAT KIND OF EXAMPLE ARE YOU? 177
- WHEN EVIL HAS A FACE 181
- THE WAITING SEASON 183
- SUFFERING! 186
- GOD KEEPS HIS PROMISES! 189
- THE TAPESTRY OF BITTERNESS 193
- SURRENDING ALL 196
- BROKENNESS 200
- SIDESHOW DISTRACTIONS 203
- LOGOS 207
- IS ANYTHING TOO HARD FOR GOD? 211
- GOD'S SOVEREIGNTY 215
- JUST UNIQUELY YOU 218
- THE D-TOOL OF SATAN: "DISCORD" 224
- THE D-TOOL OF SATAN: "DISCONTENTMENT" 227
- THE D-TOOL OF SATAN: "DISCOURAGEMENT" 231
- THE D-TOOL OF SATAN: "DOUBT" 236

SHOWERS OF BLESSINGS

When reflecting over my life and especially during my most difficult years, I see how God has never failed me, never left me, and He has never ever forsaken me. It doesn't matter the many trials and difficulties that confronted me, God was there for me and with me.

When I look into the mirror of my reflections, no matter how difficult the situation, and the impossibility of the problem being resolved, it was God who gave me the strength to get through it all. I didn't say that He removed the situation nor resolved the problem, but I did say that He gave me the strength to endure.

God is always ever-present in our lives. Pain, trouble, and problems are not foreign to Him. When Jesus walked this sinful dusty earth over 2,000 years ago, He experienced pain, faced persecutions, and ran head-on into trouble. So whatever emotional feelings I experienced, me being His child, and with His Spirit dwelling in me, I believe that Jesus was experiencing those same emotions with me. Jesus has told us in Scripture that to follow Him, we will experience suffering, but when we have endured, we shall wear a crown and have eternal life with Him in heaven. "God blesses those who patiently endure testing and temptation. Afterward they will receive the crown of life that God has promised to those who love him" (James 1:12).

When God showers us with blessings, He never holds back anything. Think for a moment. When God sends rain upon the earth, everything on earth benefits from the rain. The rain comes and refreshes and make the grounds fruitful. When I plant my flower garden, rain water has a totally different affect on my garden then regular water. It's not the same quality of water. Rain brings the needed nutrients to my garden. Just as rain provides the needed nutrients to my garden, God showering blessings on us, gives us what we need to thrive.

Our God is a very good God and He shows us through His acts, in love and goodness towards us. He showers on us infinite blessings. He opens the floodgates of Heaven and allow it to rain down on us all that is wonderful. He lavishes His blessings on us, because we are His chosen ones and His blessings should be a reminder of how important we are to Him. But we are not just important, we are His cherished possessions. We are His beloved children. His love is so great towards us that mere words cannot truly express the full capacity of God's love for us. We are the apple of His eye, "...for he who touches you, touches the apple of His eye'" (Zechariah 2:8).

When God showers us with His blessings, His blessings are fulfilling His promises to us. He showers us with His grace, mercy, love, compassion, kindness, forgiveness and so much more, each and every day of our lives. "And God is able to shower all kinds of blessings on you. In all things and at all times you will have everything you need. You will do more and more good works" (2 Corinthians 9:8).

When we have faith in God, He rains down His promises that He will never leave us nor forsake us. And He continues to shower us through His Spirit. How? The Holy Spirit is our Helper. He sanctifies us. He guides us, comfort us, teaches us, strengthens us. He helps us to do our Father's will and makes us more like Christ. The Holy Spirit changes us and convicts us, but He doesn't condemn us. "What we have received is not the spirit of the world, but the Spirit who is from God, so that we may understand what God has freely given us. This is what we speak, not in words taught us by human wisdom but in words taught by the Spirit, explaining spiritual realities with Spirit taught words" (1 Corinthians 2:12-13).

God's Holy Word (the Bible) is like the refreshing rain-water. It is essential and nourishes us. The Bible shows us God's character and provides us with God's revelation of Himself. When we read the Bible, we have a connection with God. When we neglect His Word, we will experience a drought. We miss out on important ways we hear the voice of God. We need God's Word to survive, for insight, care, love, guidance, and grace. We need the Word to refresh us, to infuse us with hope, to provide us with strength, joy and comfort. We need the Word to empower us and to direct our steps.

Only God can provide blessings upon blessings to shower down on us. God is the source of all blessings. God showers us with infinite blessings. He opens the floodgates of Heaven and rain down on us all that is good. "I will cause showers to come down in their seasons; they will be showers of blessing" (Ezekiel 34:26). We should always be thankful and appreciative for God's bountiful showers of blessings in our lives.

God showers us with Spiritual blessings as well. Paul describes those Spiritual blessings in the first chapter of Ephesians. God does not hold back nor leave out any blessings for us, "Praise be to the God and Father of our Lord Jesus Christ, who has blessed us in the heavenly realms with every spiritual blessing in Christ" (Ephesians 1:3). He chose us to be His very own, through Jesus Christ. We stand covered in God's love. God has adopted us into His own family. God's wonderful kindness and favor has been poured out on us. God showers down upon us the richness of His grace and bountiful mercies. He understands us and knows what is best for us at all times, and when the time is ripe He will gather us all together to be with Him in Christ, forever. Because of what Christ has done, we have become gifts to God, He delights in us, and we were chosen from the beginning of time.

Ooh, it's just get better and better! For God doing these mighty great things for us, we should give Him glory. And because of what Jesus did, those who believe in Him, is marked as belonging to Him by the Holy Spirit. The Holy Spirit's presence within us is God's guarantee that He really will give us all that He promised. The Spirit's seal upon us means that God has already purchased us and that is His guarantee to bring us to himself.

Glory hallelujah! Thank you Father through Jesus Christ for Your showers of blessings!

"THE I WILL GOD"

"I will make you into a great nation and I will bless you; I will make your name great, and you will be a blessing. I will bless those who bless you, and whoever curses you I will curse; and all people on earth will be blessed through you" (Genesis 12:1-3).

Before God will bless you in the abundance that He sets forth, He must first put you in a place or position to receive the blessing. I am not speaking of self-attainment nor the daily blessings that we receive. I am speaking of exceptional blessings.

The Lord told Abram to leave his country, his people, his family and friends, and go to a land that He would show him. The Lord was about to do a new thing in the life of Abram, but to receive this blessing, Abram who knew not God, but God knew him, needed him to trust Him. God commanded a step of faith from Abram. Abram must "trust and obey" God.

Showers of Blessings

Abram had to move to a far away place without the love and security he had at home. If Abram was to receive the blessings that the Lord had for him, He had to separate himself from the pagan idolatry that was known to that land and go to the land which God would show him. If Abram would step out on faith, God had made some iron-clad promises to him and God will never break a promise.

As long as Abram puts his trust in the Lord, "The I Will God" would supply all his needs. Abram responded in faith that was illustrated through his obedience by leaving all.

Let's look at the promises God made to Abraham.

"I will make of thee a great nation." From the loin of Abraham would come a great nation, a people too numerous to keep a count of. God changed Abram's name to match his destiny. The man called Abram will now take on the famous name of Abraham, "Your name will no longer be Abram; your name will be Abraham, for I will make you the father of many nations" (Genesis 17:5). This new name means "father of a multitude," matching God's revelation of what Abram would become.

"I will bless thee and make thy name great." The blessing upon the righteous is beyond the comprehension of man. The blessing that will fall on Abraham will also be passed on to his progeny, friends, and others. Our walk with God should not be a blessing thought of as solely for us, our walk should be so that others who are in our space would also receive blessings. I would not be where I am today had not other Christians had sown some of their blessings into my life.

"I will make your name great." What an awesome promise. Today, Abraham is referred to as the Father of the righteousness.

Hebrews 11:8 says, "By faith Abraham, when called to go to a place he would later receive as his inheritance, obeyed and went, even though he did not know where he was going."

"I will bless them that bless you." This is a mighty statement. When the child of God is blessed by others, means, when you do a good thing for someone or to someone, God will bless you. This is a reciprocal blessing. Yet there are people who could help others, but refuse to. Like the man in the New Testament who had an overflow of crops and his barns weren't big enough for the harvest, but rather than share with the community, he decided to tear down his barns and build bigger ones. As he was thinking to himself, God showed up and told him that "tonight he was going to die" (Luke 12:16-21). If you get nothing else out of this, make it your goal in life to share your blessing and resources with others.

"And the one who curses you I will curse." Many times the child of God will spend too much time trying to get back at those that came against them. God knows who your enemies are. Be still and let the Lord fight your battles. "No weapon form against thee shall prosper." Whenever the wicked comes at you, they can't get to you unless God allows it. Many times the Lord allow the worker of iniquity to come against us to see if we are true and faithful Christians. The tests of time, are to make us stronger, not weaker.

"All peoples on earth will be blessed through you." God will bless all the families of the earth through Abraham. This is a "worldwide blessing." How? This promise made to Abraham begins God's plan of salvation. It began to prepare God's people for salvation. It points the way forward to which Jesus, the Son of God will bless the world with salvation from sin, won by His sacrifice on the Cross, His Resurrection from the dead, and His Ascension into Heaven.

We serve a never changing God. God is the same yesterday, today, and forever. God will never forget His promises to Abraham nor will He forget His promises to us. God is still requesting that we believe in Him and we should respond in obedience and faith, because God will always fulfill His promises. What promises? There are thousands of promises already given to us by God in Scripture. God is always faithful. He is simply saying to us, "I Will" to you today and everyday, if we will just listen to Him through His Word and be obedient, trusting in His promises. How much more enriching our lives can be if we believe and obey "The I Will God!"

PROOF OF THE RESURRECTION

We live in a time when proof is needed to validate that something is right or wronged. We live in a society that demands proof. How often have you heard someone say, "prove it." Many people have lost their lives trying to prove a point.

In the legal world, there is a term that is commonly used and it is called "the burden of proof." In a legal dispute, one party has the burden of proof to show that they are correct, while the other party has no such burden and is presumed to be correct. The burden of proof requires a party to produce evidence to establish the truth of facts needed to satisfy all the required legal elements of the dispute.

The burden of proof is usually on the person who brings a claim in a dispute. The necessity of proof always lies with the person who lays charges. In criminal cases the burden of proof is on the prosecutor and the defendant is presumed innocent until proven guilty. In a civil lawsuit, the plaintiff bears the burden of proof that the defendant's action or inaction caused injury to the plaintiff.

Proof has always been and will continue to be the acceptable process. Time does not change the relevance of proof. Proof is still needed to persuade others when arguing a point.

Even today, people are demanding proof that Jesus rose from the dead. Even doubting Thomas after the disciples told him that Jesus had risen from the dead, had problems believing: "One of the disciples, Thomas, "The Twin," was not there at the time with the others. When they kept telling him, 'We have seen the Lord,' he replied, 'I won't believe it unless I see the nail wounds in his hands - and put my fingers into them - and place my hand into his side'" (John 20:24-25). Thomas required physical proof which is the best evidence for more than circumstantial.

The resurrection has been under attack, from the day Jesus left the tomb until present. Matthew tells us that the soldiers reported His resurrection to the authorities and they advised them, "Say ye, His disciples came by night, and stole him away while we slept. And if this come to the governor's ears, we will persuade him, and secure you. So they took the money, and did as they were taught" (Matthew 28:13-15). This was the great cover-up in Scripture. The Scripture does not say as they were told, but it says, "as they were taught." Which implied that they rehearsed the lie until they felt safe enough to repeat it as a TRUTH.

There are those who still seek to explain the resurrection as a purely subjective experience of the disciples. Though this took place over 2,000 years ago, it is still the centerpiece of

Christianity. Time does not dissolve a truth. Jesus told the disciples about His death and His resurrection. Listen as Luke foretells His death: "Then He took the twelve aside and said to them, 'Behold, we are going up to Jerusalem, and all things which are written through the prophets about the Son of Man will be accomplished. For He will be handed over to the Gentiles, and will be mocked and mistreated and spit upon, and after they have scourged Him, they will kill Him; and the third day He will rise again'" (Luke 18:31-33).

The disciples didn't understand any of it, just as today there are those who hear the Word, "For the wages of sin is death, but the free gift of God is eternal life in Christ Jesus our Lord" (Romans 6:23). But believe me as the old saying goes, "the proof is in the pudding." The proof for the sinner will be realized as he or she is cast into the lake of eternal fire.

Scripture gives us ample "Proof of the Resurrection:"

THE FIRST PROOF: The women came to Jesus' tomb on the first day of the week, to anoint Jesus' body with spices they had prepared. To their surprise they realized that the stone was rolled away from the door of the tomb and Jesus was not in it. Let me remind you, and keep in mind, they were not expecting what they found. I am pretty sure that while they were en route to the tomb, they probably wondered, how were they going to get into the tomb. Their hindrances didn't stop them from making an effort. Their faith and love for Jesus led them to see an improbable situation. Some of us when confronted with an improbable situation will give up before even making an effort.

Faith will remove stones that you couldn't have never imagine. These women walked by faith. If they had followed the logic of their eyesight, they would not have gone to the tomb, because the stone at the door would have kept them home, but because they went, they became the **first proof** that a resurrection had taken place.

When they entered the tomb, they did not find the body of Jesus. Two men in shining garments suddenly stood beside them and said, "Why do you look for the living among the dead? He is not here; he has risen! Remember how he told you, while he was still with you in Galilee: The Son of Man must be delivered into the hands of sinful men, be crucified and on the third day be raised again. Then they remembered his words" (Luke 24:4-8). The proof is in the pudding!

THE SECOND PROOF: The stone was not a mere rock. It was shaped and sealed for one to get in and nothing to get out. But Scripture reminds us that, "And behold, there was a great earthquake, for an angel of the Lord descended from heaven and came and rolled the boulder back and sat upon it" (Matthew 28:2). Why lose time and sleep worrying about those huge boulders in your life that you, by yourself can't move, when all you have to do is let Jesus do your heavy lifting. The stone was not rolled aside for Jesus to get out, but for the women could be **proof** as eyewitnesses to the greatest miracles of all times. The proof is in the pudding!

THE THIRD PROOF: Jesus' missing body. The guards had been posted and the area was very secure to make sure that His disciples couldn't come to steal Jesus' body. NO grave can hold Jesus. He is the first fruit. Paul says, "But now Christ has been raised from the dead, the first fruits of those who are asleep. For since by a man came death, by a man also came the resurrection of the dead. For as in Adam all die, so also in Christ all will be made alive" (1 Corinthians 15:20-22). Jesus is the first fruit of God's harvest, a harvest of living souls that will be raised to life because of the death and resurrection of Jesus, because He lives, being resurrected from the dead, we also will experience resurrection. The proof is in the pudding!

THE FOURTH PROOF: Jesus has risen. "The angel said to the women, 'Do not be afraid, for I know that you are looking for Jesus, who was crucified. He is not here; he has risen, just as he said. Come and see the place where he lay" (Matthew 28:5-6).

He conquered death! Death, is humanity's greatest enemy. Jesus was obedient to the Father, even to death. "Who, being in the very nature God, did not consider equality with God something to be grasped, but made himself nothing, taking the very nature of a servant, being made in human likeness. And being found in appearance as a man, he humbled himself and became obedient to death - even death on a cross" (Philippians 2:6-8).

He has ascended to the throne of God. "Therefore God exalted him to the highest place and gave him the name that is above every name, that at the name of Jesus every knee should bow, in heaven and on earth, and every tongue confess that Jesus Christ is Lord, to the glory of God the Father" (Philippians 2:9:11). The proof is in the pudding!

What is Jesus doing in heaven sitting at the right hand of God? He makes intercession for those that are His. "Therefore He is able also to save forever those who draw near to God through

Him, since He always lives to make intercession for them" (Hebrews 7:25). When we sin, He is our Advocate. He pleads our case before the Father, "My little children, I am writing these things to you so that you may not sin. But if anyone does sin, we have an advocate with the Father, Jesus Christ the righteous" (1 John 2:1). He is actively preparing for our heavenly arrival, "Let not your hearts be troubled. Believe in God, believe also in me. In my Father's house are many rooms. If it were not so, would I have told you that I go to prepare a place for you? And if I go and prepare a place for you, I will come again and will take you to myself, that where I am you may be also" (John 4:1-3).

SOMEBODY'S WATCHING YOU!

There was a song recorded by the singer Rockwell, released by Motown, called "Somebody's Watching Me." The song was released in 1984, as the lead single from his debut album. The first three lines of the song goes like this:

> I always feel like somebody's watchin' me
> I always feel like somebody's watchin' me
> And I have no privacy.

But are we truly being watched? Surveillance cameras are everywhere. There are cameras on homes and businesses that are watching us. Doorbell cameras are so widely used. Dash-cams are in vehicles, as back-up cameras. Body cameras are almost on every police officer in the country. Video cameras and automatic license plate readers are on top of many utility poles, street lights, city buses, mounted on school buses and let's not forget that they are on many law enforcement vehicles.

Just the other day, our local news reported on an incident that involved a death due to a hit and run accident. The suspect's vehicle was identified by obtaining surveillance footage from security cameras. Databases can correlate location data from smartphones, private surveillance cameras, license plate readers, and facial recognition software, so if law enforcement wants to track you down and know where you have been, they can.

Even when you are at home in your own privacy of your own backyard, you are being watched and recorded by multiple devices from many sources. Even on the inside of your home you don't have any privacy, especially if you have purchased some form of smart device for your enjoyment, such as a smart T.V. or Amazon Echo or Alexia, or some other smart device with speakers. My Alexia is always listening, not just for my voice commands, but every little sound that is being made in my house, including me typing this.

This is very scary knowing that something or somebody is always watching and listening to you. What a violation of privacy! But what we should be afraid of, not that man is watching us or listening to us, but that God is watching us, the All-Seeing One. For Scripture tells us that, "The eyes of the Lord are in every place, keeping watch on the evil and the good" (Proverbs 15:3). "And no creature is hidden from his sight, but all are naked and exposed to the eyes of him to whom we must give account" (Hebrews 4:13).

God is omnipotent, which means that He is all-powerful. He is omniscient, which means that He is all-knowing. He is omnipresent, which means that He is present everywhere at all times. God sees, hears, and knows everything. There is absolutely nothing that is hidden from God. God is not deaf nor blind. He cannot be bribed, manipulated, nor fooled. He knows us inside and out. "For my eyes are on all their ways. They are not hidden from me, nor is their iniquity concealed from my eyes" (Jeremiah 16:17).

God never sleeps nor slumbers. Can you imagined that! God's eyes are eternally always opened. God doesn't miss anything. Guess what? God keeps records on us. Ooh, yes He does! Scriptures says, "And I saw the dead, small and great, stand before God; and the books were opened: and another book was opened, which is the book of life: and the dead were judged out of those things which were written in the books, according to their works" (Revelations 20:12). God keeps records of every time we are obedient and disobedient.

God knows our every thought, every mistake, every seed we have ever sown, and every action. He knows our strengths and weaknesses. He knows every word that will come out of our mouths before the thought is even formed in our brains. He knows about the temptations we are exposed to, our living concerns, and what troubles us. He knows what you are fighting against and who is fighting against you. He knows our prayers before we pray. He knows what time we will wake up and the time we will fall asleep. He knows all of our business. We cannot hide anything from God. There is nothing that can stop the "all-seeing" vision of God.

God sees everything and He knows all things. God sees every act of kindness and every injustice. God has no blindspots, His view is never obstructed. God never blinks, His eyes are never half-shut nor do they close and open. God doesn't have any blinders, nothing prevents Him from understanding the full situation. God doesn't have any barriers, nothing can stop Him from going anywhere and He sees through it all.

In Psalm 139 David reveals to us how big, how awesome, how powerful, and how wise God is. God's omniscience is put on display:

> "O Lord, you have examined my heart and know everything about me. You know when I sit or stand. When afar you know my every thought. You chart the path ahead of me, and tell me where to stop and rest. Every moment, you know where I am. You know what I am going to say before I even say it. You both precede and follow me, and place your hand of blessing on my head.

This is too glorious, too wonderful to believe! I can never be lost to your Spirit! I can never get away from my God! If I go up to heaven, you are there; if I go down to the place of the dead, you are there. If I ride the morning winds to the farthest oceans, even there your hand will guide me, your strength will support me. If I try to hide in the darkness, the night becomes light around me. For even darkness cannot hide from God; to you the night shines as bright as day. Darkness and light are both alike to you.

You made all the delicate, inner parts of my body, and knit them together in my mother's womb. Thank you for making me so wonderfully complex! It is amazing to think about. Your workmanship is marvelous - and how well I know it. You were there while I was being formed in utter seclusion! You saw me before I was born and scheduled each day of my life before I began to breathe. Every day was recorded in your Book" (Psalm 139:1-16).

God doesn't have any eye ailments: thyroid eye disease, age-related macular degeneration, astigmatism, cataracts, glaucoma, diabetic retinopathy, blurred vision, double vision, amblyopia, color blindness, nor floaters. No, none of those. He has x-ray microscopic 20/20 vision. God sees everything and in every detail. He sees every event in the world and every detail of our lives, until the end. He can see ALL things, and He does!

1,440 MINUTES

Each day has 1,440 minutes in it, and yet there are times there appears to be not enough minutes in a day. You wake up every morning ready to tackle the day or you may plan your day the night before, but by the end of the day you realized that you didn't accomplish most of things you needed to do. You find yourself asking the question, "Where did the time go?" It is a question I asked myself, most days.

Each day has 1,440 minutes in it. No one can control the time, but everyone can control how they use their time. Scripture tells us, "Look carefully then how you walk, not as unwise but as wise, making the best use of the time, because the days are evil. Therefore, do not be foolish, but understand what the will of the Lord is" (Ephesians 5:16-17).

Each day has 1,440 minutes in it. But do you ever find that you are too busy for a daily chat with God? When we allow our schedule to make us too busy, this draws us away from God. It's time to take a long look at your priorities and values. When organizing your daily schedule, organize your life around one simple principle, "God comes first." "Commit your work to the Lord, and your plans will be established" (Proverbs 16:3).

Each day has 1,440 minutes in it. How do you place God in your life? Place God where He belongs - as the Head of your life and the very center of your day and life. Scriptures tells us, "But seek first the kingdom of God and his righteousness, and all these things will be added to you" (Matthew 6:83). God needs to be the #1 priority in our lives. God doesn't want to have to compete for attention for a spot on your long list of things to do. God wants a relationship with you. He wants you to spend time with Him. He wants you to talk to Him, to tell Him about your weaknesses, your failures, victories, problems, or whatever is on your mind. "O my people, trust him all the time. Pour out your longings before him, for he can help?" (Psalm 62:8)

There are 1,440 minutes in a day. How many of those minutes are you going to spend with God? The unnecessary time you spend on Social Media, some of that time could be dedicated to God. It doesn't matter what time of day we spend with God, He just wants us to take time out of each day to talk to Him. "Seek the LORD and his strength; seek his presence continually" (1 Chronicles 16:11).

I know that your days are extremely busy, but you can find quality time to spend with God. While taking a shower you could have a praise-fest going on. You can talk to Him while getting dressed, commuting to work or back home. You could talk to Him while exercising, doing the dishes, while cooking, doing laundry. You could talk to Him before getting out of bed or if you wake up in the middle of the night. It doesn't matter how long you talk to God, as long as you do. Not rushed or feeling obligated, but a sincere candid conversation, like talking to your best friend.

God is available twenty four hours a day and seven days a week. He is always available and He is never too busy to engage with us. You can talk to Him at anytime, any place, anywhere, and at all times. He is a great listener, an excellent helper, and the very best friend you will ever have. There is 1,440 minutes in a day, how many minutes of the day will you spend talking to your Bestie? "Pray all the time. Ask God for anything in line with the Holy Spirit's wishes. Plead with him, reminding him or your needs, and keep praying earnestly for all Christians everywhere" (Ephesians 6:18).

THE GOD OF THE IMPOSSIBLE

The Bible tells us numerous times that "Nothing is impossible with God." We are encouraged to believe that ALL things are possible with Him. The angel told Mary that God intended for her to bear His Son, the angel proclaimed, "Nothing will be impossible with God" (Luke 1:37).

We serve a God that specializes in the impossible. He deals so well with impossibilities. Whatever the impossibility is, God will show up right on time. He is never too late to do what He needs to do. When the impossible is brought to Him, in full faith, the circumstances of the impossible MUST be accomplished by God, if God is to be glorified.

The things that are on your mind, the things in your heart that are beyond your ability to see how they can be fixed, can be fixed by God. Nothing is impossible with God! God sees things differently than we do, and He can bring about things in ways you could never imagine, all for your good and for His glory.

When reflecting over your life, you have faced some unusual circumstances, made some bad choices, and a few mistakes, but it was never too late for God to deal with your situation, triumphantly. When you present your case to God in full surrender and trust Him, no matter what you are going through, remember this, God can "restore...the years that the locust hath eaten" (Joel 2:25). God heals and restores and there is nothing too hard for Him.

No matter what we have to face, our God loves us. Scripture tells us over and over again how much God loves us. Nothing escapes the All-Seeing God. Even when it seems that God is silent, He is working things out for our good and for His glory. Isaiah says, "O Jacob, O Israel, how can you say that the Lord doesn't see your troubles and isn't being fair? Don't you yet understand ? Don't you know by now that the everlasting God, the Creator of the farthest parts of the earth, never grows faint or weary? No one can fathom the depths of his understanding. He gives power to the tired and worn out, and strength to the weak. But they that wait upon the Lord shall renew their strength. They shall mount up with wings like eagles; they shall run and not be weary; they shall walk and not faint" (Isaiah 40:27-31).

Our ways are never hidden from the Lord. God sees and knows every detail of our lives. He knows when we are tired, hungry, hurting, distressed, mistreated, lonely. God is ever vigilant and ever sustaining. It is God that provides us strength in our weakness, because even the strongest of the strong can grow weary. God's children gains strength because He strengthens them.

Cecilia D. Porter

Scripture tells us, "I can do all things through him who strengthens me" (Philippians 4:13). There is nothing too hard for God!

Showers of Blessings

The Bible is the truth and the truth sets you free. Nothing is impossible with Christ. God tells us not once, but many times and He shows us repeatedly in many stories within the Bible, that nothing is impossible with Christ. But there is something that we must do first, Mark 9:23 says, "And Jesus said to him, 'If You can?' All things are possible to him who believes." Yes, you know that He existed, died on the cross, and was resurrected, so that we may have salvation, but knowing Him as in having a relationship with Him is a whole different thing. It is when you truly know Him that your faith can function in its fullness.

When you know that you have a relationship with Him, it is then that you can believe that all He wants is the best for you, including those dreams and hopes that have been shattered. "For I know the plans I have for you, declares the Lord, plans to prosper you and not to harm you, plans to give you hope and a future" (Jeremiah 29:11). God is the Dream Maker and He makes all things possible. We just have to trust God by faith, and then rest in Him. Remember, regardless of what it looks like, God is working out everything for your good and for His glory. We serve a God that specializes in the IMPOSSIBLE!

LIVING IN THE MOMENT

So many people do not live in the moment. Why? Maybe because they spend each moment of their everyday life, looking and visiting their pass or focusing on their future.

Living in the moment means letting go of the past and not waiting for the future. To live in the moment means to be attentive to the present moment. To live in the moment means not dwelling on the past, nor being anxious or worried about the future.

Life is a journey in which we travel down the road of uncertainty and many unpredictabilities. Now there will be some turbulent storms along the way and many roads filled with potholes in them, but that's life.

Sometimes we get so caught up in our past, focusing on past mistakes and bad choices, that we miss the specialness of each moment afforded us during the day. We become so focus on the past that we can't appreciate the opportunities that God is offering us now, in the present. When you are living in the past you can't enjoy the present. It's okay to reminisce, but to remain in the land of would'a, should'a, could'a is very unhealthy. Scripture tells us, "A glad heart makes a happy face; a broken heart crushes the spirit" (Proverbs 15:13).

Living in the past will have you focused on those unfortunate moments and past toxic relationships. Living in the past and holding on to the guilt for the mistakes you made isn't going to do you any good. Stop blaming yourself for everything that went wrong in your life. Beating yourself up over past mistakes are not going to change anything. No amount of guilt can erase the mistakes you made in the past. It's time to move on, forgive yourself and start enjoying each day of your life, in each moment of your life. The Bible says, "...though the righteous fall seven times, they rise again..." (Proverbs 24:16a). Everyday is a new day. You may fall, but you will rise again.

Quoting from Dalai Lama, "There are only two days in the year that nothing can be done. One is called yesterday and the other is called tomorrow, so today is the right day to love, believe, do and mostly live." There are many reasons to live in the moment. Life unfolds only in moments. Living in the past or living in the future only, is not living in the moment, because they only exists as thoughts only. You have to let go of what you thought should have happened and live in what is happening now. That's living in the moment.

We must be grateful for each and every moment. Ecclesiastes 3:12-13 says, "...there is nothing better than to be happy and enjoy ourselves as long as we can. And people should eat and drink and enjoy the fruits of their labor, for these are gifts from God."

Living in the moment means to enjoy life while you can. How exciting would it be to live every moment to the max. You still have not experienced your greatest moment yet. It's time to enjoy your life, taking one moment at a time.

OUR ARCH ENEMY #1

In one of my favorite movies, was centered around the 1930's during Prohibition. Featuring in it was the notorious gangland kingpin Al Capone, who supplied illegal liquor and controlled nearly all of Chicago. Bureau of Prohibition agent Eliot Ness had been tasked with halting Capone's activities, but his first attempt at a liquor raid failed due to corrupt policemen alerting Capone. He then encounters veteran officer Jimmy Malone, who opposed the corruption and offered Ness some help by suggesting they find a man from the police academy who had not been under Capone's influence and still believed in law enforcement. Because of George Stone's superior marksmanship and integrity, they recruited him. Oscar Wallace was an accountant from Washington, D.C., he was also assigned to Ness. They successfully raided Capone liquor warehouse and started to gain some positive publicity, the press dubbed them as, "The Untouchables." Al Capone became the team's "Arch Enemy #1."

The Untouchables, with its star Eliot Ness, was about how hard Ness had to fight and to defeat one of his most fiercest enemies, Al Capone. You know what got me about Capone, was that he didn't just killed innocent people, but he also killed the very ones who was suppose to be loyal to him. He was ruthless and he did not love or care about anyone at all.

Now when I thought about this movie, I couldn't help but think about another Capone that we have to deal with on a daily basis. This person doesn't wear a tailored made suit and smoke expensive cigars, even though he will occasionally show up in a suit or sometimes a dress. This person has been around for centuries. This person that we have to deal with doesn't just operate and live in a fictional world, but this person will show up all over the world. This person is so slick that he may show up in your home to cause trouble in your marriage, trouble with your children, and trouble in your family.

Oh no, he just doesn't stop there. He will show up on your job causing you all kinds of trouble, misery and grief. He will even try to get you fired and make sure that you become unemployed. He may even show up at your family reunion where he will cause family members to hate one another.

You want to know what is absolutely crazy, he will even show up at church on Sunday mornings where he will try to distract you from listening to God's message, distract you from worshipping the Lord, distract you from going to Sunday School, distract you from attending Bible Study, distract you from coming to Church, or most importantly, he will try to distract you from having a relationship with Jesus.

In real life, our "Arch Enemy #1" doesn't have to be a person, appearing as a man, a woman, a boy, or a girl. No! Our enemy can use all kinds of things to come against us, such as drugs, alcohol, unclean magazines, movies, or books. He may show up in a song or any other device that will negatively influence you to do the wrong things.

Our "Arch Enemy #1" is very deceiving, very conniving, very crafty, very heartless, and very evil. This person that I am talking about is Satan himself. Scripture tells us, "Be sober, be vigilant, because your adversary the devil, as a roaring lion; walketh about seeking whom he may devour" (1 Peter 5:8).

In the Bible Satan is known by many different names:

> In John 14:30, he is known as the prince of this world.
>
> In Matthew 13:19, he is known as the wicked one.
>
> In John 8:44, he is known as the murderer and the father of lies.
>
> In 2 Corinthians 6:15, he is known as Belial.
>
> In Revelation 9:11, he is known as the angel of the bottomless pit Abaddon (Hebrew), and Apollyon (Greek).
>
> In Ephesians 6:12, he is known as the Ruler of darkness.
>
> In Matthew 12:43, he is known as the unclean spirit.
>
> In 2 Corinthians 4:4, he is known as the god of this world.

In Revelation 12:10, he is known as the accuser.

In 1 Peter 5:8, he is known as the adversary and roaring lion.

In Matthew 12:24, he is known as Beelzebub the prince of the devils.

In Matthew 4:1, he is known as the devil.

In Ephesians 2:2, he is known as the prince of the power of the air.

In Revelation 12:9, he is known as the deceiver of the whole world, great dragon, old serpent, Devil, and Satan.

Satan, our "Arch Enemy #1" desires to destroy us. We must "resist him" through our Christian faith, and this can only be done as we regularly "submit to God" by studying His Word daily, by being obedient to Him, and by living in His will. It is through the shelter of God that we can have safety from our "Arch Enemy #1." When are trapped into worldly thinking and the concerns of this world, that's when our enemy takes advantage of us. But Christians who are filled with the Spirit of God and walks in the light through Scripture cannot fail, although Satan continues to throw his fiery darts at us, and great satanic storms still comes against us.

Yes, we are Christians who are living in our Arch Enemy's world, but victory is surely ours as believers in Jesus Christ, who lives in God's will, and through our Christian walk. Guess what? I have some good news for you. Our "Arch Enemy #1" has already been defeated. Jesus won the victory over him through the cross and the resurrection. The ultimate defeat of Satan is when he will be condemned to the lake of fire forever.

THOSE THAT LOVES GOD

How much do you love God? Scripture tells us, "And thou shalt love the Lord thy God with all thy heart, and with all thy soul, and with all thy mind, and with all thy strength: this is the first commandment" (Mark 12:30). We could never do this in excess, because we could never love God too much. In our daily walk and devotion, we can love Him deeper. Our love for God can become richer, but our love could never be too excessive. However deep your love for God is, believe me, His love for you is greatly deeper. Your love for Him can't come close to the intensity of affection and devotion our Father has for us.

The Bible says, "But if one loves God truly [with affectionate reverence, prompt obedience, and grateful recognition of His blessing], he is known by God [recognized as worthy of His intimacy and love, and he is owned by Him]" (1 Corinthians 8:3).

Can you handle the truth? God loves us profoundly! Even before He made the world, God loved us and chose us in Christ. He has blessed us in Christ with every spiritual blessing in the heavenly realms. He predestined us for adoption, as His through Jesus, according to His will and purpose. This is a doctrine to rejoice in and to be enjoyed. He totally delights in us. His love for us is beyond human understanding.

I have the receipts! There are so many passages in the Bible that are devoted to loving God. God tells us the promises of loving Him and how He will bless those who love Him:

* "And if you will carefully obey all of his commandments that I am going to give you today,

and if you will love the Lord your God with all your hearts and souls, and will worship him,

then he will continue to send both the early and late rains that will produce wonderful

crops of gain, grapes for your wine, and olive oil. He will give you lush pastureland for

your cattle to graze in, and you yourselves shall have plenty to eat and be fully content"

(Deuteronomy 11:13-15).

* "Because he has loved Me, therefore I will deliver him; I will set him securely on high, because he has known my name" (Psalm 91:14).

* "Come and have mercy on me as is your way with those who love you" (Psalm 119:132).

* "The Lord is fair in everything he does, and full of kindness. He is close to all who call on

him sincerely. He fulfills the desires of those who reverence and trust him; he hears their

cries for help and rescues them. He protects all those who love him, but destroy the wicked" (Psalm 145:17-20).

* "The one who obeys me is the one who loves me; and because he loves me, my Father will love him; and I will too, and I will reveal myself to him" (John 14:21).

* "And we know that God causes all things to work together for good to those who love

God, to those who are called according to His purpose" (Romans 8:28).

* "That is what is meant by the Scriptures which say that no mere man has ever seen, heard

or even imagined what wonderful things God has ready for those who love the Lord" (1 Corinthians 2:9).

* "Happy is the man who doesn't give in and do wrong when he is tempted, for afterwards

he will get as his reward the crown of life that God has promised those who is tempting

him, for God never wants to do wrong and never tempts anyone else to do it" (James 1:12).

These are just a few passages from the Bible. The Bible has many more passages devoted to those that loves God. But no matter how much we love God, He loves us so much more. We have no idea the magnitude of God's love for us. He loves us completely and unconditionally. "And I pray that you, being rooted and established in love, may have power, together with all the saints, to grasp how wide and long and high and deep is the love of Christ, and to know this love that surpasses knowledge -- that you may be filled to the measure of all the fullness of God" (Ephesians 3:17a-19). We can't even comprehend how massive God's love is. His love cannot be fully explained, but I am thankful that I can experience it.

I am so thankful for God's love for me and I am also thankful that He knows all about me. "O LORD, you have searched me and you know me. You know when I sit and when I rise; you perceive my thoughts from afar. You discern my going out and my lying down; you are familiar with all my ways. Before a word is on my tongue you know it completely, O LORD. You hem me in -- behind and before; you have laid your hand upon me. Such knowledge is too wonderful for me, too lofty for me to attain" (Psalm 139:1-6).

The fact is, God knows us intimately and deeply. He knows every little detail about our lives. We are never out of His sight. We are never out of His mind. There is no time or never will be a time, when His eye is off you. His attention can never be distracted from you. There is no greater love than this!

God knows what troubles us, and what trials we are going through. He knows every time you stump your toe and every tear you shed. He knows every one of your aches and pains. He knows when you lie down and when you are awake. He knows when you are depressed, lonely, and disappointed. When you shedded those tears, because of the lost of a loved one, He was there crying with you. He knows when you are irritated and He sees you when you are in despair. He knows exactly how you feel every second of each day. He knows every single strand of hair on your head.

How amazing is that! Do you know what else amazes me? How we don't have nothing to offer God and yet He loves us anyway.

We bring absolutely nothing to the table. Yet He loved us way before we learned to love Him. God is love! We can always rely on the love God has for us. You know what else is amazing? There is absolutely nothing that can ever separate us from God's love. Paul says, "For I am convinced that neither death, nor life, nor angels, nor principalities, nor things present, nor things to come, nor powers, nor height, nor depths, nor any other created thing, will be able to separate us from the love of God, which is in Christ Jesus our Lord" (Romans 8:38-39).

When you really love God, there will be some things that you will desire to do. You will desire to have a deep and personal relationship with Him. Those that loves God will desire to know Him intimately. To love God is to worship and praise Him. To love God is to desire Him. To love God is to put Him first in your life. To love God requires a will to obey Him. If you really desire a closeness with Jesus, He wants to give it to you. Jesus tells us that He will make Himself known in a special way to those that love Him.

"If anyone acknowledges that Jesus is the Son of God, God lives in him and he in God. And so we know and rely on the love God has for us. God is love. Whoever lives in love lives in God, and God in him" (1 John 4:15-16).

"Eye has not seen, nor ear heard, nor have entered into the heart of man the things which God has prepared for those who love Him" (1 Corinthians 2:9).

IF ONLY

Have you ever had the "If Only" blues? "If only" is used when you start thinking and saying that you would like a situation to be different. It is a way of saying you are sorry or regret something. Regret is a feeling of sadness about something sad or wrong or about a mistake that you have made, or something that you have done or not done. We all make mistakes and we all do things or have done some things that we regret. Sometimes you reflect what would have happened if I had made a different choice or taken a different path. Whether in a current relationship, past relationship, a job opportunity or a missed opportunity.

We go through a mental revolving door of, "if only." If only I had studied harder. If only I had written that number down. If only I had known what to do in that situation. If only I had made that investment. If only I lived closer to my family. If only I had taken better care of myself. If only I could have been there. If only I had done this of that. If only the clock could turn back the hands of time. "If only," of course is a wishful dream. Not for the past as it was, but for the present that could have been, if only the past could have been a little different, then my present situation could be a little bit better.

"If only" was on the minds of Lazarus' family. All that and more is in Martha's "if only" to Jesus as he arrives in Bethany. When Martha came to Jesus and saw Him, she fell at His feet and said, "Lord if you had been here, my brother would not have died" (John 11:21). She probably knew that it had taken Jesus at least two days to get there. Lazarus had already been dead for a few days, but perhaps he might just had made it in time..."if only."

Jesus tells her that "her brother shall rise again." Martha agrees that it will happen "in the resurrection at the last day." But Jesus responded with His own Great Confession "I am the resurrection, and the life; he that believe in me, though he were dead, yet shall he live, and everyone who lives and believes in me will never die" (John 11:25-26).

Jesus is challenging Martha and is urging her to change her "if only" for an "if Jesus." If Jesus, the One that is the way, the truth, and the life. If Jesus, the Messiah, the One who was promised by the prophets, the One who was to come into the world as the Light of the world. If Jesus, God's own Son, the One in whom the living God that created everything that exists. If Jesus, the resurrection in person, and life to come, where nothing is too hard for Him or impossible. If Jesus, our Advocate, Deliverer, King of kings, Lord of lords, God of gods, Redeemer, Savior, Supreme Creator over all. Then why should there be any "if only?"

Showers of Blessings

Sometimes we get stuck in the past. There are times when all we can think about is, "if only." It's easy to linger in that place, to stay on the road of "if only" and let our anger simmer or fall in a state of despondency or depression. Wondering, "if only" doesn't change what has already happened. Even though it's a hard thing to acknowledge mistakes and wrong choices in life, but being stuck in the land of "if only" doesn't remove the hurt or pain or the grief. If you are feeling like that and if you have an "if only" in your heart or mind, run off to meet Jesus. Tell him your problem. It's okay to ask Him like Martha, "why didn't You come sooner" or why He allowed that awful thing to happen in your life?

Then be prepared for the surprise factor. There is no way to predict how God will respond to you, because Jesus always works in mysterious ways. The good news is that Jesus will respond to you. Jesus will meet your "what if" and "if only" problem with some new part of what God has for your future, that will only burst into your present, whatever that, "if only" is troubling you, with renewed hope and unlimited possibilities that will be greater than you could ever imagined. Scripture tells us, "Eye has not seen, nor ear heard, nor have entered into the heart of man the things which God has prepared for those who love Him (1 Corinthians 2:9). You can't even imagine that possibilities of what God has in store for you. "If only" you could imagine that!

SEEING GOD IN EVERYTHING

When we learn to see God in everything, we will see and experience calmness and peace. We will see how He takes His peace and places It in us. When we experience His indescribable peace, what was dark and gray now becomes so vividly colorful.

The sorrow we may be experiencing, may or may not be removed. Our circumstances, may or may not be changed. The suffering and difficulties, may or may not cease. But Jesus, the Lord and Master of our life, can take that sorrow, pain, discomfort, grief, mistreatment, and gloom, and can give us a song of deliverance, even in the midst of our trials.

Nothing can happen to you, unless God allows it. That persecution you are going through, God allowed it. God will allow someone to turn your life completely upside down, and when that happens, He commands for us to love them, and to pray for them: "But I tell you, love your enemies and pray for those who persecute you" (Matthew 5:44). Those who mock you, persecute you, lie on you, or despitefully use you, they are considered to be your enemies. Jesus says that we are blessed when we experience these things. He tells us that there is a new way to live our life: with love, not hate. He has already informed us that our true enemy is Satan, "For we wrestle not against flesh and blood, but against principalities, against powers, against the rulers of the darkness of this world, against spiritual wickedness in high places" (Ephesians 6:12). He tells us how to resist him, "Therefore put on the full armor of God, so that when the day of evil comes, you may be able to stand your ground, and after you have done everything, to stand" (Ephesians 6:13).

We know that God will sometime use pain and difficulty in our lives to bring blessings to our lives. So whatever God brings to your door, regardless of how terrible, horrible, dreadful, grim, or frightful it may be, His dealings with us is for our spiritual gain, even in the midst of bereavement, sorrow, and pain. Only when you are able to see God in everything, then you will understand, and learn to love them that mistreat you, with patience. When you see God in everything, those who troubles you, you know to pray for them. When those who makes your life so dark and gray, prayer leaves revenge and justice to God. Those that bring you pain, sorrow, discomfort and gloom, when you place them in God's hand, you release the power they have over you.

We must learn to see God as the One who is All Powerful and All Mighty. With the power God has as the Creator and Ruler of the universe, He is the only ONE who can perform miracles, forgive sins, and give eternal life. You can be sure that His wisdom can never err, His power can never fail, His love for you will never change.

When you can see God in everything, then you will understand that God is the fabric of your life and He has colored it, painted it, with all the colors of His Spirit, showing love and kindness, and every heavenly thing above.

SINGING THE BLUES

If you are feeling blue, that means you are feeling sad, gloomy, depressed, dour, sullen, downhearted, unhappy, weary, moody, just in the dumps.

The use of the color blue to mean sadness goes all the way back to the 1300s. Some sources points to Geoffrey Chaucer as the first author to write the word blue to mean sadness. In his poem, Complaint of Mars from around the year 1385, he writes: "Wyth teres blewe and with a wounded herte" which translates to, "With tears blue and with a wounded heart."

In Greek Mythology, Zeus was the sky and thunder god. He ruled as king of the gods of Mount Olympus. It was said that when he was angry, he would create a strong storm so that it would threaten life on earth. But when he was sad, he would make it rain while the sky was still blue.

As surprising as it is, blue is associated to tears and sadness. The feeling of desperation cause by sadness adds up to the phrase of "feeling blue." People when feeling blue will usually say: "I am feeling so blue today." Or "The weather is so gloomy that it is making me feel blue." Or "That music is making me so sad, so blue."

Blues Music is a type of music which was originated by African American in the Deep South, in work songs and spirituals. Blues songs incorporates spirituals, work songs, field hollers, shouts, chants and rhymed narrative ballads. The Blues, as a musical style, come out of the hardship of everyday living. They express the hones feelings of those who experience lives of struggle and difficulty. In the midst of Covid-19 with its many variances, then you add the outbreak of Monkeypox, and many of us are "Singing the Blues."

Singing the Blues is nothing new to the children of God. Many of our Biblical heroes have song the blues. Take Elijah for example. When Elijah fled from Queen Jezebel, he went to Beersheba and left his servant there, then he went a day's journey into the wilderness, he sat down under a juniper tree, and prayed that he might die. He then journeyed for 40 days and 40 nights until he reached Mount Horeb, and there he went into a cave and spent the night. God asked Elijah, "What are you doing here, Elijah?" He replied, "I have worked very hard for the Lord God of the heavens; but the people of Israel have broken their covenant with you and torn down your altars and killed your prophets, and only I am left; and now they are trying to kill me, too" (1 Kings 19:9-10).

In Psalm 77, Asaph was truly "Singing the Blues." He writes, "I cry to the Lord; I call and call to him. Oh, that he would listen. I am in deep trouble and I need his help so much. All night long

I pray, lifting my hands to heaven, pleading. There can be no joy for me until he acts. I think of God and moan, overwhelmed with longing for his help. I cannot sleep until you act. I am too distressed even to pray! I keep thinking of the good old days of the past, long since ended. Then my nights were filled with joyous songs. I search my soul and mediate upon the difference now. Has the Lord rejected me forever? Will he never again be favorable? Is his lovingkindness gone forever? Has his promised failed? Has he forgotten to be kind to one so undeserving? Has he slammed the door in anger on his love?" (Psalm 77:1-9).

Some people maybe feeling like Elijah and Asaph, singing the blues, and questioning whether God has left you without any help in your time of need. God revealed Himself to Elijah, not in a great wind or earthquake or fire, but in a still small voice. God revealed that Elijah was never alone. He wanted Elijah to know that He had been there all along and He had 7,000 in Israel who hadn't bowed nor kissed Baal.

Asaph cried out to God for courage during a time of deep distress. His plea was, "I need help." The source of Asaph's distress was his doubt. Only after he put aside his doubts about God's holiness and care for him did he eliminate his distress. I am sure that Asaph didn't reach this particular emotional place overnight. There is always a progression from our emotional experiences. Despair usually begins with disappointments. Disappointments usually leads to doubt. Doubts usually will lead to depression. Then from depression, despair is birth. Disappointment is the Mother to despair.

We will have circumstances that will disappoint us. Disappointments will bring you to a point of despair. Jesus promised us that He will never leave us nor forsake us. God has never broken a promise, so what makes you think He will in your case.

Many times God is at work in our lives and we just can't see his footprints, but He is working for us and for our good. There will be numerous circumstances over which you will have no control and from which you cannot remove. But you must remember that your circumstance is never what they appear on the surface to be. We do not know what miraculous events God is orchestrating through our situation. We are supposed to just trust Jesus. Scripture tells us, "And we know that all that happens to us is working for our good if we love God and are fitting into his plans" (Romans 8:28).

WEEDS OF LIFE

When I was working in my flower garden pulling out weeds, my thoughts regarded the weeds as unwanted guests. Weeds are the enemy in my garden. They are never wanted, never invited, and is a thorn in my side. No one likes to deal with weeds, and weeds must be rooted out, or they will out compete with my flowers.

Weeds are aggressive and often are quicker than plants at reproducing and spreading. They steal and rob the moisture and nutrients from the plants. Weeds grow rampantly. The best way to get rid of them is knowing how to identify them. The number one rule with weeds is, you never let them take seed. But as Christians how many weed seeds do we allow to take root in our lives? Those weeds are choking out our Spiritual fruit. In your spiritual garden, are you nurturing and watering weeds or Spiritual fruit?

Cecilia D. Porter

Scripture tells us the difference between fruit and weeds. Galatians 5:22-24 says, "But the fruit of the Spirit is love, joy, peace, patience, kindness, goodness, faithfulness, gentleness and self-control. Against such things there is no law. Those who belong to Christ Jesus have crucified the sinful nature with its passions and desires." We should be investing in these types of fruit, because anything else are weeds.

Scripture also helps us identify what are weeds, "The acts of the sinful nature are obvious: sexual immorality, impurity and debauchery, idolatry and witchcraft; hatred, discord, jealousy, fits of rage, selfish ambition, dissensions, factions and envy; drunkenness, orgies, and the like. I warn you, as I did before, that those who live like this will not inherit the kingdom of God" (Galatians 5:19-21).

Whatever you nurture and water will grow. If you are nurturing weeds, they will choke out the fruit. Weeds hinders fruit from maturing. Jesus explains to us in Matthew 13:22, that the the seed that fell among the thorns, who was the Christians that heard the Word of God, but the cares of this world and its deceitfulness of wealth choked the Word, making it unfruitful. These things are weeds.

Our Spiritual life is a sort of flowerbed or garden, and like all flowerbeds and gardens, there will be some weeds that will pop-up in our lives. We all must deal with some type of weed management. How? By identifying the weeds and pull out all weeds in our life. Weeds are acts of the sinful nature. Colossians 3:5 says, "Away then with sinful, earthly things; deaden the evil desires lurking within you; have nothing to do with sexual sin, impurity, lust and shameful desires; don't worship the good things of life, for that is idolatry."

Weeds are destructive! So pull out the weeds! They damage our Spirit and choke-out our faith, our Spiritual motivation, and causes us not to focus on Spiritual things.

MY CROSS TO BEAR

"How I plead with God, how I implored his mercy, pouring out my troubles before him. For I am overwhelmed and desperate, and you alone know which way I ought to turn to miss the traps my enemies have set for me. There's one - just over there to the right! No one gives me a passing thought. No one will help me; no one cares a bit what happens to me. Then I prayed to Jehovah. 'Lord,' I pled, 'you are my only place of refuge. Only you can keep me safe. Hear my cry, for I am very low. Rescue me from my persecutors, for they are to strong for me'" (Psalm 142:1-6).

Sometimes we tend to think that other people's lives are so easy. Like they don't have a care in the world. We look at their life and they appear to be living on Easy Street. Their life appear to be so easy and carefree. We begin to think, "If only my life could be so easy," or "If only I could be like them," or "Why is my life filled with so much sorrow and pain?" We wonder, "Why is my cross so heavy when everyone else's cross seems to be so light?"

One person's cross (life) can look ooh so beautiful, filled with rich jewels and covered in gold. The other person's cross (life) may look like it's covered with beautiful flowers. Sometimes we envy those who are rich with their golden cross covered with jewels, but we don't know how heavy their cross may be. We don't know their story nor could we walk in their shoes. That person whose life seems so lovely and covered with beautiful flowers, beneath those flowers could be some piercing thorns, that are tearing at their skin.

Just the other day I read a story titled, "Is Your Cross Too Heavy To Bear," and I would like to share it with you:

> A young man was at the end of his rope. Seeing no way out he dropped to his knees in prayer. "Lord, I can't go on," he said. "I have too heavy a cross to bear." The Lord replied, "My son, if you can't bear its weight, just place your cross inside this room. Then open that other door and pick out any cross you wish." The young man was filled with relief. "Thank you Lord," he sighed, and he did what he was told. Upon entering the other door, he saw many other crosses, some so large the tops weren't even visible. Then he spotted a tiny cross leaning against the far wall. "I'd like that one Lord," he whispered. And the Lord replied, "My son, that is the cross you just brought in." (Source unknown)

God knows best what cross we can bear. We don't know how heavy other people's crosses are. If you could try on other people's crosses, thinking that their cross is lighter than yours, you would discover that not one of them will suit you as well as your own. Our cross is meant just for us. We need to stop comparing our cross to someone else's cross.

In life you will experience tribulation, trouble, and trials. We become so focused on how large and heavy our cross is and how tired we are from carrying our cross, that we can't see God's outstretched hand reaching out to help us carry our own cross. That painful hardship, whether it is short-term or permanent, is out of our control. We should always keep our eyes and hopes in God, and believe that He can see us through anything. We have a God that is always watching over us. Our God is Omnipotent, which means He is all-powerful. He is Omniscient, which means He is all-knowing. He is Omnipresent, which means He is all-present. God is aware of our every one of our circumstances, and He is aware of the heaviness of our cross.

That cross you are caring is not meant to hinder, hurt, or wound you. God is using that cross to get you where you need to be. He is helping you reach your God given destiny. It is called God's Divine Providence. Our greatest growth often comes during our most difficult moments. One thing I want you to know, without a cross to bear, you will never reach your full potential nor receive that mind blowing blessing that God has prepared for you.

The Lord will never give you a cross or situation that you can't handle. He never promised us that we can have the opportunity to pick our own cross, but He did tell us that He would help us bear it. God will never put more on you than you can bear.

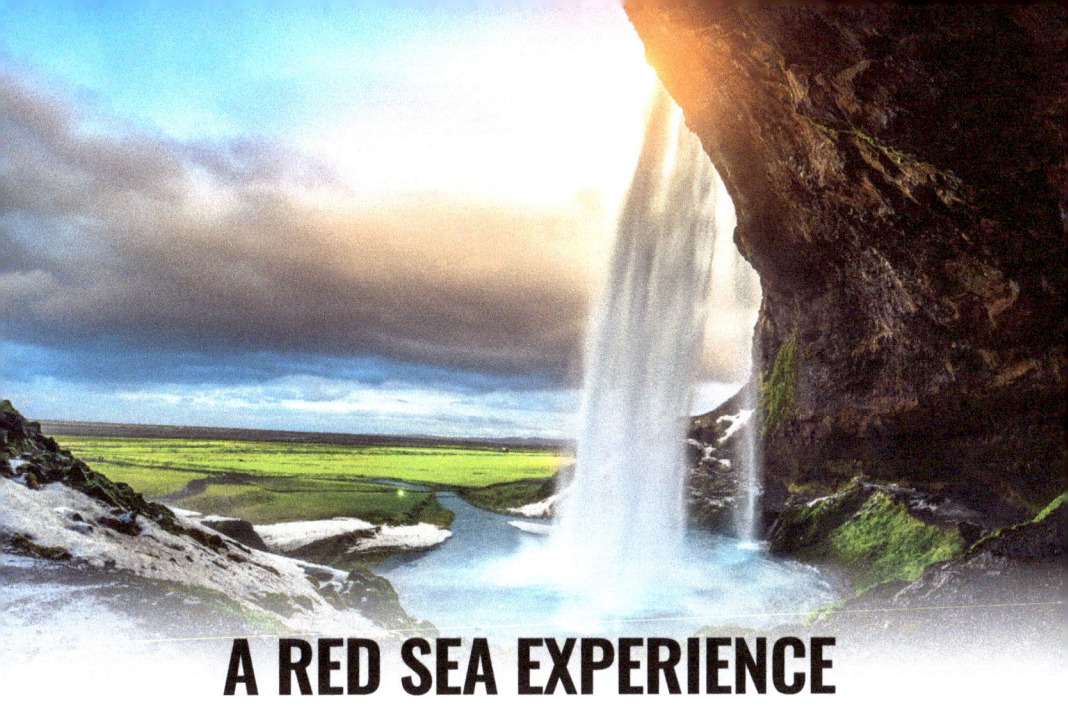

A RED SEA EXPERIENCE

Our life's journey comes with a lot of hard situations. Sometimes we are faced with situations that drains our peace and joy. It could be a challenging relationship, a financial crisis, health issues, or a host of other things. Whatever it is, we somehow just can't see our way out of the situation. Many situations and challenges are put before us as a "test of faith." I am a person of faith, and I believe that God can make a way out of no way. The same God we read about in the Bible is the same God that we serve today.

Take the story of Moses when him and Aaron went to Egypt to confront Pharaoh to let the children of Israel go. So God had to teach Pharaoh a lesson. Ten plagues were brought down on Egypt and Pharaoh finally released the Israelites. When they left Egypt, God led them along a route through the Red Sea wilderness. They camped in Etham, at the edge of the wilderness. Pharaoh and his army pursued the people of Israel. The Israelites were trapped in front of the Red Sea with no way out. But Moses told them to not be afraid, just stand still and watch the wonderful way the Lord would rescue them that day. He wanted them to know that the Lord will fight for them and they wouldn't have to lift a single finger. God purposefully led them to that exact spot, with no options of escape of their own, because He wanted them to see HIS power and He wanted all Egypt to know that He was Jehovah. God told Moses to stretch out his rod over the sea. Moses did what the Lord commanded, and the Lord opened up a path through the sea and the water was divided. The Lord caused a strong east wind to blow, drying the sea bottom and the people crossed over on totally dry ground. Isn't God amazing! When all the Israelites were on the other side, God told Moses to stretch out his hand again over the sea, so that the waters would come back over the Egyptians. Moses did and the Egyptians drowned in the sea.

No one wants to be in a "Red Sea" situation. But sometimes we find ourselves in situations where we have to trust God to make a way out of no way. We have to wait and trust Him to deliver us in difficult and troubling times. I have had some experiences where I had no way out, but God made a way out of no way for me. He opened a path for me that I couldn't have possibly opened for myself. I have had some mind-blowing experiences, and each time my faith was put to the test, and out of each of those experiences, my faith was restored and strengthened. Nothing is impossible for God, and God will always provide a way, even when it seems impossible.

For the last few years, I have found myself feeling very defeated. Sometimes I am depressed, downright discouraged, and overwhelmed. How so, do you ask? Well, I have been in a situation that I can't do nothing about. I am waiting on God to part the sea for me, so that I can walk through on dry ground, to get to the other side. I need God to tell me which direction to take; so I stand, watch, and wait. It seems that my enemies are all around me, and it seems that they are closing in on me, but I have to hold on to my faith and trust the will that God has for my life. While I am watching and waiting, I have learned something very valuable. I just need to be still and watch God get His glory. This battle isn't mine, it's the Lord's, because I know that only God can delivered me from this situation. He actually brought this situation to my front door. I am at a place where I can't see any way out, not through my own power, anyway. I know that God is with me and that He is leading me and guiding me. I need to remember that God is always there for me.

Sometimes, He leads you to just be still. Simply wait, but we look at waiting as being stuck. We wait, but we don't do it gracefully. We want God to deliver us now, the very minute we are faced with our "Red Sea Experience." We don't want to face those raging seas in our lives. We want the water to part immediately so we can walk through on dry ground, but we can't do this until we stand still. We need to stand still and remember that God led you to this place for a reason. If we stand still we will see the salvation of the Lord. Scripture reminds us to, "Trust in the Lord with all your heart; do not depend on your own understanding. Seek his will in all you do, and he will show you which path to take" (Proverbs 3:5-6).

Showers of Blessings

Standing still is so very hard to do. Waiting on God to clear the pathway for us isn't easy. How do I know if God is waiting on me to do something first or am I waiting on Him? What a test of faith! So many questions floods your mind. We question what is taking God so long to open up the pathway. We began to question God. Is God really moving on our behalf? We are constantly looking for some signs from God. God is always leading us, some ways are subtle and some are obvious.

If you are having a "Red Sea Experience" don't panic. God is always with you. He promised that He would never leave you nor forsake you. Remind Him of His promises to you. No matter what situation you may be in, God is with you. He is leading you. It may seem as though that nothing is happening at all, but at God's appointed time, He will reveal His will to you. God wants to lead you in a divine direction that will give you an abundant life, but it takes trusting Him with all of your heart. The Lord says, "I will guide you along the best pathway for your life. I will advise you and watch over you" (Psalm 32:8).

WHO IS WAITING ON WHO?

WAITING! Waiting, and yet still waiting. We have to wait all the time. We have to wait for our food to be prepared. We have to wait in traffic. We have to wait for our test results. We have to wait on someone to return our telephone call. We have to wait in line at the grocery store. We have to wait for all sorts of things. We even have to wait until we fall asleep.

Sometimes we often think of "waiting" when we are waiting on God to answer our prayers, fulfill His promises, and awaiting a blessing of some kind. In our season of waiting we will often use the phrase, "I am waiting on God." Which usually means that we are waiting on Him to do something for us. What are we waiting on God to do for us? We are waiting on Him to avenge us, to lead us, to direct us, to provide for us, to heal us, to answer a prayer, to reveal His glory, to do only what God can do.

God's concept of time is not like ours. We as humans are creatures of time, because our lives revolves around time. God is the Creator of time. "With the Lord, a day is like a thousand years, and a thousand years are like a day" (2 Peter 3:8). God's time is different from our time.

God has everything about our lives already planned. His timing is perfect. At the proper time, God has already determined that something will happen. He is never late nor is He ever too early. No one can rush Him to do anything before its time.

We are always saying that we are waiting on God, but do we ever think that maybe God is waiting on us? Isaiah 30:18 says, "And therefore the Lord [earnestly] waits [expecting, looking, and longing] to be gracious to you; and therefore He lifts Himself up, that He may have mercy on you and show loving-kindness to you. For the Lord is a God of justice. Blessed (happy, fortunate, to be envied) are all those who [earnestly] wait for Him, who expect and look and long for Him [for His victory, His favor, His love, His peace, His joy, and His matchless, unbroken companionship]!"

Realizing the possibility that not only are we "waiting on God" - maybe God is waiting on us. The Lord earnestly waits for us "expecting, looking and longing to be gracious" to us. For those who earnestly wait for Him, who expect and look for Him. For what? For His victory, His favor, His love, His peace, His joy, and His matchless unbroken companionship. This is what we are waiting for in one form or another. Whatever we are waiting on God for, it can surely fall into that description.

We are waiting and God is waiting. He is waiting for us to get into the position for the outpouring of His blessings. God is waiting to bless us beyond our wildest dreams and expectations. He knows the issues of our hearts. Are you prepared to receive the blessings that you are longing for?

"Then you will call upon Me, and you will come and pray to Me, and I will hear and heed. Then you will seek Me, inquire for, and require Me [as a vital necessity] and find Me when you search for Me with all your heart" (Jeremiah 29:12-13). When? "...when you search for Me with all your heart."

GOD'S DIVINE PROVIDENCE

Divine providence is God's governance over the affairs of mankind and their destiny. He directs and watches over everything in the universe, ensuring that His will, will be accomplished here on earth. He has specific plans for our lives and He orders things in our lives to make sure that our destiny is fulfilled. Our destiny isn't left to mere chance. "Known unto God are all his works from the beginning of the world" (Acts 15:18).

God is the Creator of the universe and He rules over all creation - nature, animals, people, and nations. Since God is the Creator of heaven and earth, everything that occurs in the universe takes place under His Divine Providence. That means that everything happens under God's sovereign guidance and control. God governs everything in the universe as our loving father. Scripture tells us, "And we know that all things work together for good to them that love God, to them who are the called according to his purpose" (Romans 8:28). "All things" means, "All things." God never loses control of anything! If God lose control of anything, that's "All things," then He is not sovereign, and that means that He is not God.

Through God's divine providence, He accomplishes His desired will. To ensure that His purposes are fulfilled, God governs the affairs of man. Most times we can't see God's guiding hand of providence while He is guiding us, but we mostly can see it in retrospect. In Scripture, we see so many examples of God's divine providence. The story of Joseph shows God's divine providence. From the actions of his brothers, to the malicious acts of Potiphar's wife. Then Joseph's understanding of interpreting dreams, placed him in a position for the preparation for the famine. God's divine providence saved Israel and some Egyptians.

Ruth is another case of God's divine providence. She finds herself in Boaz's field, they become husband and wife, then parents, and then great-grandparents of King David. God works in mysterious ways. There are so many more examples of God's divine providence in the Bible. How God perfectly orchestrated His will for so many lives.

God's divine providence means that He cares about every little detail of His creations. He not only care about the big things, He also cares about the tiniest of things. He notice and cares about everything. Listen to the words of Jesus, "Are not two sparrow sold for a penny? Yet not one of them will fall to the ground apart from the will of your Father. And even the very hairs of your head are all numbered. So don't be afraid; you are worth more than many sparrows" (Matthew 10:29-31). Nothing escapes God, including senseless accidents and tragedies. If you are having some testing experiences, well thank God, for you are in the company of God's saints listed in Hebrews and how God wonderfully provided for them. There were some who were tested to the limit and yet they remained faithful. They knew that their providential God would not abandoned them. Daniel was thrown in the lion's den and he trusted in God. The three Hebrew boys were thrown into the fiery furnace and yet they trusted in God.

Basically, providence means, the first seven letters of the word itself -- p-r-o-v-i-d-e. God will always provide for us, because He is our Provider. Providence means that God is aware of everything that happens in our lives. He is invested in us and because He has invested in us, he guides us, motivates us, comfort us, clarify things for us, and helps us make the best decisions. God is our Provider. Things do not happen randomly, but purposefully. There is not a day that we will not face some type of challenge. Those challenges comes in different sizes and shapes. God places those tests before us simply to bring us to a place where He can effectively use us. With every challenge God will provide a provision. God will never ask you to do something that He will not enable you to do. We will never see the hand of God move on our behalf until we step out beyond our own abilities and challenge God's Word. Where God guides, He provides. God provides the Promise. God provides the Plan. God provides the Power. God provides the Purpose. God provides the Provision. God provides the Protection. God provides His Presence.

GOD'S INESCAPABLE PRESENCE

God is omnipresent. Omnipresent describes something "existing or being everywhere at the same time, constantly encountered, widespread, common." Literally, God's omnipresence means that God is present everywhere.

Have you ever played the game of Hide-and-Seek? Hide-and-seek is a children's game in which one player closes his or her eyes for a brief period, counting to a certain number (usually to 100), while the other players hide. The "seeker" opens his or her eyes and tries to find the other players, called the "hiders." The first one found is the next "seeker" and the last one found is the winner of that round.

Do you think that some people try to play Hide-and-Seek with God? There were a few people in the Bible who thought they could play Hide-and-Seek with God:

Adam and Eve tried to hide from God. They were forbidden to eat from the Tree of Good and Evil, but they were disobedient and ate from it anyway. As the results of their disobedience, from eating from the tree, their eyes were opened: "And they heard the sound of the Lord God walking in the garden in the cool of the day, and the man and his wife hid themselves from the presence of the Lord God among the trees of the garden" (Genesis 3:8).

Jonah tired to hide from God. God called him to go and preach to the people of Nineveh, "Go to the great city of Nineveh and give them this announcement from the Lord: 'I am going to destroy you, for your wickedness rises before me; it smells to highest heaven'" (Jonah 1:2). Jonah tried to hide from the Lord. He headed for Tarshish, went down to Joppa, and boarded a ship. The Lord caused a great wind in the sea, Jonah was thrown overboard, and a great fish swallowed him. He was inside the fish for three days and three nights before the fish vomited him up.

Now since our God is everywhere present, how can anybody try to think that they can hide from His presence? David provides us with one of the greatest statements ever about God being omnipresent. Listen to what he wrote:

"Where shall I go from your Spirit? Or where shall I flee from your presence? If I ascend to heaven, you are there! If I make by bed in Sheol, you are there! If I take the wings of the morning and dwell in the uttermost parts of the sea, even there your hand shall lead me, and your right hand shall hold me. If I say, 'Surely the darkness shall cover me, and the light about me be night,' even the darkness is not dark to you; the night is bright as the day, for darkness is as light with you" (Psalm 139:7-12).

David knew that God knew him inside and out, and he pondered where in the world could he hide from the Lord, even if he ascended to heaven, descended to hell, if he went east, west, north or south, to the farthest part of the seas, even to hell itself -- it would not matter, because the Lord is everywhere.

No matter where we go, no matter where we are, God is always present with us. Even if we can't sense His presence, He is always with us. He is always present wherever we go and wherever we are, 24 hours a day, seven days a week. We never have to make an appointment with Him. We never need to be placed on His calendar. He is never too busy to hear us when we pray. He is never preoccupied with other people's problems that He can't attend to our problems. You will never receive a message from an angel of God, delivering a message that God is too busy handling someone's else crisis and not be able to handle yours.

God's presence is like the air that we breathe. Air is invisible. Air is tasteless. Air is odorless. Although we can't see it, taste it, nor smell it, it exist, because we can't live without it. We depend on air for our very existence. In the same way, we can't see God, and we often don't realize that He is present with us, yet He is always there, everyday, no matter what, just like the air that we breathe.

God is ever present in our best times and our worst times. He is with us in the midst of our suffering, sickness, pain, grief, divorce, betrayal, cancer, accidents, death, abuse, war, and even in our moment of death. He is there in our celebrations, healing, marriage, victories, in new relationships, old relationships, all relationships, new homes, new jobs, new births. God is always present in our lives. He is completely available to us no matter where we are, no matter what time of day, God sees us and hears us. No matter what!

"He knows about everyone, everywhere. Everything about us is bare and wide open to the all-seeing eyes of our living God; nothing can be hidden from him to whom we must explain all that we have done" (Hebrews 4:13).

THIS IS ONLY A TEST!

The Emergency Broadcast System (EBS), sometimes called the Emergency Broadcasting System was an emergency warning system used in the United States. The system was established to provide the President of the United States with an expeditious method of communicating with the American public in the event of war, threat of war, or grave national crisis. In later years, it was expanded for use during peacetime emergencies at the state and local levels. Although the system was never used for a national emergency, it is used for civil emergency messages and warnings of severe weather hazards.

When the announcement comes on the television or radio, normal programming would be suspended with one of the following announcements:

* This is a test. For the next sixty (or thirty) seconds, this station will conduct a test of the Emergency Broadcast System. This is only a test.

* This is a test. This station is conducting a test of the Emergency Broadcast System.

This is only a test.

* This is a test of the Emergency Broadcast System. The broadcasters of your area in voluntary cooperation with the FCC and other authorities (or, in later years, federal, state and local authorities) have developed this system to keep you informed in the event of an emergency.

There were a number of variations for the second half of the statement. During the system's early days, stations other than the designated station for an area were required to shut down in the event of an emergency and the message was a variation of: "If this had been an actual emergency, you would have been instructed to tune to one of the broadcast stations in your area."

Life is full of tests. You have to take and pass tests while you are in elementary, middle, and high school. In high school while you are in your favorite class, scanning your syllabus, you see that there are going to be two major tests, a mid-term and a final. You have to take and pass tests to finish high school. You have to take a test to get into college. You have to take a test to enter a Master's Program. You have to take and pass a test to drive a car. To gain employment you have to take a job aptitude test. To obtain employment you have to take and pass a drug test. You even have to take and pass a test to obtain a life insurance policy. Did you know that life is a test?

God ordains tests in our lives, not for His sake, but for ours. God will allow trials and tribulations to come our way and He will use these trials as a way of testing us. Unfortunately, we do not get the option of choosing our tests. God has made us many promises in the Bible, but we have never been promised a life without trials, tribulations, and tests. We are promised a God that will walk with us and will give us strength during those difficult times in our lives.

We serve the same God today, that our biblical faith-walkers did in their days. Joseph was sold into slavery by his brothers. He worked for Potiphar and because of his wife's lies he was thrown into prison. God granted Joseph a very special gift, to interpret dreams. His gift of interpreting dreams elevated him to become the second highest ranking officer in Egypt. Can you not imagine the heaviness of the tests that Joseph faced? Joseph trusted the promises of God. He knew that God had a plan for his life. He endured the difficulties because of his faith in God.

Moses spent time in God's presence and God used Moses mightily. He was an instrument of God to lead the children of Israel out of Egypt. But there were so many trials along the way. The Israelites just whined, grumbled, and complained. Moses was so frustrated with them he asked God, "Why pick on me, to give me the burdens of a people like this" (Numbers 11:11). Moses had enough of their whining and complaining that he told God, "If you are going to treat me like this, please kill me right now; it will be a kindness! Let me out of this impossible situation" (Numbers 11:15).

Showers of Blessings

Job lost his houses, his wealth, his livestock, and his children, yet he chose to praise God for His goodness during his test. Job said, "I came naked from my mother's womb, and I shall have nothing when I die. The Lord gave me everything I had, and they were his to take away. Blessed be the name of the Lord" (Job 1:21). The Bible said, "In all of this, Job did not sin or revile God."

There are so many other great examples of our Biblical faith-walkers who were confronted with all kinds of tests, and many trials and tribulations, but through their faith, they became more than conquerors. Scripture tells us, "Count it all joy, my brothers, when you meet trials of various kinds, for you know that the testing of your faith produces steadfastness. And let steadfastness have its full effect, that you may be perfect and complete, lacking nothing" (James 1:2-4).

Whatever your test maybe, know this, God has chosen you to take that test. Pass the test and God will promote you to the next very special chapter in your life. If you flunk the test, you will have to retake it over and over again, or be forced to settle with God's second best plan He has for your life. Our lives are being tested in so many ways. If your test is about a relationship, God has chosen you to take that test. If your test is about a financial crisis, God has chosen you to take that test. These tests reveals what is truly in our hearts. Only the tests can reveal the heart and where we stand with God. The Bible tells us:

> "The heart is deceitful above all things, and it is exceedingly corrupt: who can know it?
>
> I, Jehovah, search the mind, I try the heart, even to give every man according to his

ways, according to the fruit of his doings" (Jeremiah 17:9-10).

"A good man brings good things out of the good stores up in his heart, and an evil

man brings evil things out of the evil stored up in his heart. For the mouth speaks

what the heart is full of" (Luke 6:45).

Taking the tests is half of the journey, because we must pass the tests in order to be made ready for our destiny, "God will bless you, if you don't give up when your faith is being tested. He will reward you with a glorious life, just as he rewards everyone who loves him" (James 1:12).

> PRESSED OUT OF MEASURE AND PRESSED TO ALL LENGTH,
>
> PRESSED SO INTENSELY IT SEEMS BEYOND STRENGTH.
>
> PRESSED IN THE BODY AND PRESSED IN THE SOUL,
>
> PRESSED IN THE MIND TILL THE DARK SURGES ROLL
>
> PRESSURE BY FOES, PRESSURE BY FRIENDS,
>
> PRESSURE ON PRESSURE TILL LIFE NEARLY ENDS.
>
> BLESSED PRESSURE, PRESSED INTO KNOWING NO HELPER BUT GOD.
>
> PRESSED INTO LOVING THE STAFF AND THE ROD.

Showers of Blessings

PRESSED INTO LIBERTY WHERE NOTHING CLINGS,

PRESSED INTO FAITH FOR IMPOSSIBLE THINGS.

PRSSED INTO LIVING A LIFE IN THE LORD,

PRESSED INTO LIVING A CHRIST LIFE OUTPOURED.
                                (Author unknown)

The blessing is in the pressing and the pressing is the test. Praise God from whom all blessings flows!

THE DELAYED PRAYER DEPARTMENT

Have you ever found yourself lost and confused while you wander around in the Delayed Prayer Department? You have petitioned God and your request for that particular blessing has not materialized yet. You are so tired. So frustrated. So anxious. You are overwhelmed with waiting. Days have turned into weeks, weeks have turned into months, and sometimes months have turned into years. You find yourself wondering why is God making me wait for so long? You may sometime feel, "Has God forgotten about me?"

The Bible is full of stories of people having to wait on God, such as Abraham, Job, Moses, Elijah, Joseph, and David, just to name a few, and there are countless others. They all went through some very trying and difficult times, but God always came through for them. The process of God and waiting on His promises appears to be a "Test of Faith." Sometimes God will allow us to enter into some very discouraging and traumatic situations, for the primary purpose of "testing our faith."

So what do you do while waiting on God to answer your prayers? While being in the Delayed Prayer Department, there are some things to do while you wait. One of those things is to wait for God quietly. "It is good that a man should both hope and quietly wait for the salvation of the Lord" (Lamentations 3:26). "For God alone, O my soul, wait in silence, for my hope is from him" (Psalm 62:5). There are times when you can't find the right words to say to God. But you can go to God without words and simply let yourself have some alone time with Him. I have learned that I don't always need to talk to God to pray. I can simply wait silently for Him, and with Him. I discovered this way of communing or silently waiting for God, when I was so broken after the death of my husband. There was times when I couldn't find any words to say, I just wanted to be in God's presence. I needed Him to comfort me. So I would just sit quietly, focusing on Him and His awesomeness. I enjoy the silent moments I spend with God.

While being in the Delayed Prayer Department, you must wait for God patiently. King David said, "I waited patiently for the Lord; He inclined to me and heard my cry" (Psalm 40:1). As we wait patiently for the Lord, the Lord assures us that our wait for Him will not be in vain. There are benefits from waiting on the Lord patiently. Waiting patiently on God means, trusting Him, depending on Him, looking unto Him for our help, longing for Him, counting on Him, thereby resting in Him. You will be blessed while patiently waiting on God, "Blessed is the man who trusts in the Lord, and whose hope is the Lord" (Jeremiah 17:7). You will receive His goodness while patiently waiting on God, "The Lord is wonderfully good to those who wait for him and seek him" (Lamentations 3:25).

While waiting on God in patience, we need to spend time with Him and in His Word. Patience is a Fruit of the Spirit and it can only be developed under trials. God wants us to grow, so He stretches us and while He stretches us, He strengthens us. He comforts us and He is with us giving us His grace to see us through. So while you wait, please do not worry, nor become frustrated. You are suppose to rest in God, through faith.

While being in the Delayed Prayer Department, you must wait for God expectantly. "Why are you in despair, O my soul? And why have you become disturbed within me? Hope in God, for I shall again praise him For the help of His presence" (Psalm 42:5). To wait for the Lord expectantly, is waiting in anticipation with assurance that something will happen. When a woman becomes pregnant, we say that she is expecting. She usually has to wait for nine months in expectation for her baby. She is assured that she will hold and love her baby. We wait on the Lord trusting His plan for our lives and His desire for us. We wait on the Lord in faith. We wait expecting God to answer our prayer in His timing and in His way.

God is 100% trustworthy. God loves for us to wait on Him expectantly. This means that we have placed our trust in Him. When we trust Him, with expecting anticipation, He does "exceedingly abundantly" more than we could ever think of or dream of. He will answer your prayers in a way that you could never ever have possibly imagined. God truly knows how to exceed our expectations. Just wait and see!

"Now to him who is able to do immeasurably more than all we ask or imagine, according to his power that is at work within us" (Ephesians 3:20).

SUFFICIENT GRACE

"Three different times I begged God to make me well again. Each time he said, 'No. But I am with you; that is all you need. My power shows up best in weak people.' Now I am glad to be a living demonstration of Christ's power, instead of showing off my own power and abilities" (2 Corinthians 12:8-9).

Paul was preaching to the people of Corinth. They were thinking like so many people today, that they were self-sufficient, and they boasted about it. Paul wanted them to know that all of their boasting was of foolishness. He told them that he have had some awesome visions, experiences, and revelations from the Lord. He let them know that those experiences were worth bragging about, but he was only going to boast about how weak he was and how great God is, and he would use such weakness for God's glory.

He spoke about a thorn in his side and that he had asked God to remove it three times, but God wouldn't take it away. God told him, "No. But I am with you; that is all you need. My power shows up best in weak people." Paul told them that he knew it was all for Christ's good, he was quite happy about "the thorn," including insults, hardships, persecution, and difficulties, for when he is weak, then he was strong, the less he had, the more he depended on God.

What is grace? We often define "grace" as "underserved favor" or as "unmerited favor and not getting what you deserved." Romans 3:23-24 states, "Yes, all have sinned; all fall short of God's glorious ideal; yet now God declares us 'no guilty' of offending him if we trust in Jesus Christ, who in his kindness freely takes away our sins." Grace is what inclines God to give gifts that are free and undeserved to us sinners.

Life is full of trouble. We are often faced with one disaster after another. Everybody will face some type of struggle. Sufficient grace means that God gives us enough grace, and He supplies us with as much grace that we will need, to help us face whatever situation that confronts us. He gives us enough grace to face our illness, financial needs, our rebellious children, hardships, persecutions, insults, relationship problems, or whatever troubling situation that confront us. Whatever your needs, you can rest assuredly, that God's grace will be sufficient for everything that you may lack and everything that is lacking within you.

Whatever grace you need, you can make an inexhaustible, never-ending withdrawal from Jesus' National Bank of Grace. There God's grace is in super-abundance and can never be depleted. Where you are deficient, God is sufficient. You cannot do nothing on your own. So let go and let God handle it, and experience God's transforming power in your life. His love is unlimited and His grace cannot be measured.

Three times God told Paul, no. God told him that His grace was sufficient for him, and His power was made perfect in weakness. God isn't just talking about Paul's weakness, but about yours and mine as well. If you love Jesus, you will have trials, you will have trouble, you will be tested, you will have tribulations. James 1:12 states, "Happy is the man who doesn't give in and do wrong when he is tempted, for afterwards he will get as his reward the crown of life that God has promised those who love him."

Grace is God's amazing power, where He applies His own goodness and His own resources to our lives. His grace saves us, keeps us, enables us, delivers us, justifies us, sanctifies us, and glorifies us. God is unendingly gracious towards us. Everything given to us by God is by His grace and this grace comes through Jesus Christ. John 1:16 says, "We have all benefited from the rich blessings he brought to us - blessing upon blessing heaped upon us."

In Jesus Christ, we have the complete package, in whom we have all things pertaining to life and godliness. Through the Holy Spirit, He fills us with all strength, comforts us, and give us the fullness of God. This complete spiritual package enables us to do all things through the power of Jesus Christ. Our sufficiency is from God and it is God who gives us Sufficient Grace. He constantly reminds us, "My grace is sufficient for you for power is perfected in weakness."

JESUS' PEACE

Jesus offers us free gifts, and one such gift is His peace. Jesus gives us His peace all the time. That's twenty-four hours a day, seven days a week, without any exceptions. Jesus' peace is unlike anything on earth. Jesus gives us heavenly peace, that's spiritual peace. Scripture reminds us, "But the Helper, the Holy Spirit, whom the Father will send in my name, he will teach you all things and bring to your remembrance all that I have said to you. Peace I leave with you; my peace I give you" (John 14:26-27).

When Jesus ascended to heaven, Jesus sent us His Holy Spirit and He brought peace with Him. The Spirit of Christ came to us from the Father. Jesus is the "Prince of Peace." God is a God of people and He fills us up with His peace. Jesus came to give us peace. He is the only source of peace. It is in God's perfect peace where He offers us a complete package of success, fulfillment, wholeness, harmony, security, and well being. You know that experience when we say, "It is well with my soul." That feeling that you cannot find the words to explain, because it cannot be described by words. Jesus is the only reason we can truly live peacefully with God and others.

What about having peace with my enemies? Scripture says, "But I say unto you, Love your enemies, bless them that curse you, do good to them that hate you, and pray for them which despitefully use you, and persecute you" (Matthew 5:44). God wants us to have peace with each other, even when it seems impossible to have peace with certain individuals, but it is possible. Jesus makes it possible to establish peace with one another and with our enemies. Jesus can take that enemy and turn it from a foe to a friend. Instead of the enemy fighting against you, Jesus can fix it that you will suddenly find yourself fighting side by side, and on each other's side. Proverbs 16:7 says, "When the LORD takes pleasure in anyone's way, he causes their enemies to make peace with them." I have seen it happen on many occasions. Jesus offers something that money can't buy - peace with other people, including your enemy.

Jesus offers us this wonderful free gift of peace. He said, "Peace I leave you; my peace I give to you. Not as the world gives do I give to you. Let not your hearts be troubled, neither let them be afraid" ((John 14:27). Jesus is telling us that receiving this wonderful gift is a choice. When you allow Him to take complete control over your life, you are allowing Him to take control over your fears. That's when you have given Him your troubles. When you let go and let God, He gives you His peace in exchange.

Whatever is troubling you, give it to Jesus, "Do not be anxious about anything, but in everything, by prayer and petition, with thanksgiving, present your requests to God" (Philippians 4:6). Family, financial setbacks, illness, job insecurities, and many other things will fill you with anxiety. There are some situations and problems that are inescapable, but whatever you may be experiencing, you can experience the peace of God in the midst of it all. The key is "prayer and petition." When you turn to God, through prayer, you are communing with Him, which will result in something absolutely wonderful. That sweet fellowship with God will leave you revived and refreshed. When you petition Him concerning your needs and concerns, God will infuse you with His presence, as peace. The peace of God shelters us from our anxiety and thoughts and His peace will guard your heart: "And the peace of God, which transcends all understanding, will guard your hearts and your minds in Christ Jesus" (Philippians 4:7).

The peace that Jesus gives us is beyond comprehension. It is a peace that comes from trusting God and believing that all will be well, even when it isn't. It is a sense of resting in God, knowing that you are in the middle of a storm, but also knowing that you have an Anchor. The peace that Jesus offers us is the kind of peace that steadies us in the storms. His kind of peace sustains us. It is having peace when everything seems out of control. It is the kind of peace that helps you get through the hard times, and when life takes a turn for the worse. It is a kind of peace that helps you face hardships, helps you endure conflicts, broken relationships, and other things we have to learn to live with.

Yes, you will experience difficulties in your life, that's inevitable. But when anything or anyone threatens to disturb your peace, God will keep your heart and mind at peace. In order to live in peace, you must have peace. Jesus made peace. He is our peace. God has given you His peace. You can accept it or reject it. It's your choice. Now, may peace be with you and your family.

FRUIT OF THE SPIRIT

"Fruit" normally means the seed-associated fleshy structures (or produce) of plants that typically are sweet or sour and edible in the raw state, such as apples, bananas, grapes, lemons, oranges, and strawberries. In botany, the term "fruit" in everyday language, are nuts, beans pods, corn kernels, tomatoes, and wheat grains.

As a Believer in Christ, you have been gifted with the Holy Spirit, which enables you to bear "fruit." The Holy Spirit is God, just like God the Father and God the Son. He is equally associated with the other members of the Trinity. The Holy Spirit lives inside of us. Scripture describes the Holy Spirit in personal terms, not as an impersonal force. He possesses emotions, intellect, and will. The Bible says that He teaches, guides, comforts, and intercedes for the Believers in Christ. The Believer who is indwelled by the

Spirit is also indwelled by God. The Holy Spirit possesses the attributes of deity, such as omniscience, omnipresence, and omnipotence. Whatever God can do, so can the Holy Spirit do, such as creating, regenerating, and sanctifying.

The Holy Spirit brings conviction to the unbeliever, causing him or her to see the truth of the gospel. Those who respond to this conviction and place their faith in Jesus Christ receives eternal life and a new nature. The Holy Spirit controls the believer who yields to God and submits themselves to God's Holy Word. When this happens the Believer will live in the power of the Spirit and will produce the fruit of the Spirit.

What is the "fruit of the Spirit?" Galatians 5:22-23 says, "But the fruit of the Spirit is love, joy, peace, patience, kindness, goodness, faithfulness, gentleness, and self-control." Paul says that when the Holy Spirit controls our lives, He will produce this kind of fruit in us. Before Paul talked about the "fruit of the Spirit" he talked about the fruit that comes from our sin. We all have natural evil desires and we can't ignore them. In order for us to follow the Holy Spirit's guidance, we must deal with them. How? By nailing them to Jesus' cross. The will of the Holy Spirit is in constant opposition to our sinful desires. The two are on opposite sides of the spiritual battle.

The Spirit produces character traits, not specific actions. We can't go out and do these things, and we can't obtain them by trying to get them. If we want the "fruit of the Spirit" to develop in our lives, we must develop the characters that are found in Jesus. We must learn to know Him, love Him, remember His commands, obey Him, imitate Him. Please note that "fruit" is the word used and not "fruits," love, joy, peace, patience, kindness, goodness, faithfulness, gentleness, and self-control is a whole package. We don't get some fruit and not all of it. All of theses are the "fruit" of a life lived for Jesus and guided by the Holy Spirit. A life filled with the Spirit of God will produce "fruit" that is sweet and will draw people to God. God doesn't produce sour fruit that will turn people away from Him.

The sour fruit is the sin in our lives and are the works of the flesh. "Now the works of the flesh are evident: sexual immorality, impurity, sensuality, idolatry, sorcery, enmity, strife, jealousy, fits of anger, rivalries, dissensions, divisions, envy, drunkenness, orgies, and things like these. I warn you, as I warned you before, that those who do such things will not inherit the kingdom of God" (Galatians 5:19-21). Now if you at one time fall into a fit of anger, envy, or jealousy, that doesn't mean that you will automatically be excluded from God's kingdom, but that you are living your life according to the flesh and not the Spirit.

The moment you accepted Jesus Christ as your personal Savior, you received the gift of the Holy Spirit. Then the Almighty God, God the Spirit, begins to take over and begins to change your life. Paul says, "But I say, walk by the Spirit, and you will not carry out the desire of the flesh. For the flesh sets its desire against the Spirit, and the Spirit against the flesh; for these are in opposition to one another, so that you may not do the things that you please" (Galatians 5:16-17). Walking by the Spirit is living a Spirit-filled life. If you are born of the Spirit, you have the power of the Spirit working in you. The work of the Spirit will change you. You have the power of heaven available to you to help you live a life that is pleasing to God. Live your life daily depending on the Holy Spirit's power.

SALVATION

What is Salvation? Salvation, also called deliverance or redemption, is the "saving of human beings from sin and its consequences, which include death and separation from God" by Jesus Christ's death and resurrection, and the justification following this salvation. The simplest definition of salvation is, to be delivered (or rescued) from the deadly clutches and eternal effects of sin.

When thinking about salvation, we need to understand what are we saved from, what are we saved to, and who are we saved by. The Bible clearly tells us that apart from Jesus Christ, we are condemned, "Whoever believes in him is not condemned, but whoever does not believe is condemned already, because he has not believed in the name of the only Son of God" (John 3:18). Scripture tells us that Jesus paid for our sins when He died on the cross and that means that we are no longer condemned, but is rescued from ALL condemnation, "There is therefore now no condemnation for those who are in Christ Jesus" (Romans 8:1).

So what are we saved from? We are saved from eternal damnation. Hell. Hell is mentioned over a 100 times in the Bible. It is sometimes called Hades, Abaddon, Sheol, the pit of Abyss, everlasting punishment, the abode of the dead, the inferno, the nether regions, eternal damnation, perdition, hellfire, fire, and brimstone. In Luke 16:19-31, Jesus tells the story about a certain rich man, and a beggar named Lazarus. Lazarus laid at the gate, full of sores, begging to be fed with the crumbs from the rich man's table. It came to pass that Lazarus died and was carried off by the angels into Abraham's bosom. The rich man died also, and was buried, and in hell he lifted his eyes, being in torment, and saw Lazarus in Abraham's bosom. The rich man cried out to Abraham to have mercy on him, to send Lazarus to dip his finger in water to cool his tongue, because he was being tormented in the flames. Abraham reminded him about his life, how he received the good things in life and Lazarus received evil things. Now Lazarus is being comforted and he was being tormented.

Hell is a complete separation from the presence of God. Second Thessalonians 1:8 states, "In flaming fire taking vengeance on them that know not God, and that obey not the gospel of our Lord Jesus Christ. Who shall be punished with everlasting destruction from the presence of the Lord, and from the glory of his power." This is what we are saved from!

What are we saved to? Salvation means that we are saved not only from something, which are our sins, but also for something and to someone. Salvation is a free gift that God offers us. "If the Son therefore shall make you free, ye shall be free indeed" (John 8:36). Scripture helps us to see that we have been set free. We are rescued from bondage and brought into freedom. It tells us that we are saved from God's wrath and brought into peace with God. Salvation begins to clean us and help makes us into what God wants us to be so that even when we make the slightest changes for the good, it pleases God. We can thank God that we are not what we ought to be, but we are not what we use to be either. Salvation is the first step we must all make if we want to be pleasing and acceptable to God. Jesus Christ is the Way to God, the Truth in God, and the only Life through God. No one can get to the Father without going through Jesus.

What are we saved for? We are saved to have a relationship with God. Once you recognize the Voice of God and submit to His Spirit, salvation begins to take place and cannot be stopped by anyone, any place, or anything. Salvation is not a feeling. It is a reality. Once you are saved, no one can take your salvation from you. Knowing Jesus as your personal Savior is the most exciting and important relationship you can ever have on this earth. It puts you into full and constant fellowship in your relationship with God. Salvation is the beginning of a wonderful faith related adventure with the Most High God, who is ALL-Mighty, ALL-Powerful, and ALL-Loving God! Imagine that!

The Bible speaks about Salvation in terms of the past, the present, and the future. When Jesus died on the cross for us, salvation rescued us from the penalty of sin which is death. The past is that, "It is He who saved us and chose us for his holy work, not because we deserved it but because that was his plan long before the world began - to show his love and kindness to us through Christ" (2 Timothy 1:9).

In referenced to the present, we are still in the process of being saved, "For the message of the cross is foolishness to those who are perishing, but to us who are being saved it is the power of God" (1 Corinthians 1:18).

Salvation has a future. On that day when our life will come to an end, we will be absent from the body and present with the Lord, "I tell you the truth, whoever hears my word and believes him who sent me has eternal life and will not be condemned; he has crossed over from death to life" (John 5:24). "For God so loved the world that He gave his only Son, so that everyone who believes in Him may not perish but have eternal life" (John 3:16).

Salvation is rescuing us from the principle of sin in our daily lives and our overall presence of sin while we continue to live. "But God commendeth his love toward us, in that, while we were yet sinners, Christ died for us. Much more then, being now justified by his blood, we shall be saved from wrath through him" (Romans 5:8-9). How exciting! What a mighty blessing! We Shall Be Saved!

WHY?

The WHY questions starts with us when we are children. "Why do I have to go to bed?" "Why do I have to eat my vegetables?" "Why do I have to go to school?" Even as adults, we keep asking the question, "why?" And we will continue to ask the question, "why" throughout our entire life time. "Why did God take him or her so young?" "Why the trials and tribulations of life?" "Why does this have to be my burden to bear?" "Why?" "Why?"

Why do we ask, why? Because we need to know the answer, and that is why. We ask why for a deeper understanding. If you don't have the answer for the why, just ask the question, why not? That always works. But as humans, we are curious about life. Because life's problems and situations are truly puzzling. Our brain is always in pursuit of knowledge. So why do we ask the question, why? We ask the question to acquire knowledge, to obtain a better understanding, and to eliminate the confusion.

Sometimes God never answers the "why" questions. Instead God may show us that knowing the "Who" is far more important than knowing the "why." When you realize the "Who," any "why" will be just fine. God is the Who to the why. God often tells us, the reason why, is because He says so.

Is it wrong to question God and ask Him why? Well, Moses asked God why. Moses said, "Why pick me, to give me the burden of a people like this? Are they my children? Am I their father? Is that why you have given me the job of nursing them along like babies until we get to the land you promised their ancestors?" (Numbers 11:11-12).

Job asked God why. He wanted to know, "What is mere man that you should spend your time persecuting him? Must you be his inquisitor every morning, and test him every moment of the day? Why won't you let me alone - even long enough to spit? Has my sin harmed you, O God, Watcher of mankind? Why have you made me your target, and made my life so heavy a burden to me?" (Job 7:17-20).

David asked God why. "Lord, why are you standing aloof and far away? Why do you hide when I need you the most?" (Psalm 10:1). "How long will you forget me, Lord? Forever? How long will you look the other way when I am in need? How long must I be hiding daily anguish in my heart? How long shall my enemy have the upper hand?" (Psalm 13:1-2).

Jesus asked God why, when He was on the cross. He shouted, "Eli, Eli, Lama sabachthani?" which means, "My God, My God, why have you forsaken me?" (Matthew 27:46).

We as Christians do not live a troubled free life. We often wonder why did God bring this to me? Why me? We may not understand our why's while we are in the valley, nor may we ever get an answer during our lifetime. If God decides to answer our why, we may not get the answer we desire. But whether God answers us or not, He comforts us in those dark troublesome times.

In John 9:2-3, Jesus had left the Temple and He saw a blind man whose been blind since his birth. His disciples asked him, "Why was this man born blind? Was it a result of his own sin or those of his parents?" Jesus answered, "Neither. But to demonstrate the power of God." We may never know the reason for the why, but know this, God's glory will always be displayed in our life as He molds us for His purpose.

It may not be about the "why," but maybe about the "how." How God is working out everything in our lives for His purpose and for His glory? Because we are unable to see from God's perspective. So you don't understand why your marriage didn't work. Why you are suffering from an illness. Why your love one committed suicide. Why your spouse or child is on drugs. Why you can't get a job or keep one. Why the loneliness? Why the misery? Why the unhappiness? Why the brokenness? The proverbial list of why questions are endless.

The why question can rock your faith. God has a purpose in putting us through that painful situation. Scripture tells us, "For everything comes from God alone. Everything lives by his power, and everything is for his glory" (Romans 11:36).

It's okay to ask God the "why" questions. It's God's prerogative if He chooses to answer any of them. God has never answered all of my why questions. I sometimes understand how He is working it out for me, and then there are times when nothing makes sense. As I have matured in Christ, I have learned to ask God the "what" question." "What" do you want me to learn from this experience? Then I rest in Him, because I trust Him. No matter how bleak the situation may look. No matter how hard it may appear.

The Lord is telling me to trust and follow Him. He is telling me to follow the path that He has given me. His plan is perfect for me. It may not look like it when you are in the valley. I understand that the difficulties we experience in this life, means that God is accomplishing His will in our lives. They shape us so that we may reflect the character of Christ. As we ponder the "why" question, God is simply asking, "why not you?" And He is also saying to us, "because I said so."

THE HEART

The heart is a muscle just a bit bigger than the size of your fist. It is located between the lungs, almost in the middle of the chest. It is the body's core muscle and it is the very first organ to be form in the body after conception.

With each heartbeat, the heart pumps blood through the body's cardiovascular system. When the heart beats, it makes a "lub-dub" sound. This is the sound that is made by the heart valves as they open and close. With each heartbeat, blood pushes through the aortic valve into the aorta and is delivered to the body. The heart beats about 100,000 times a day.

In the King James version of the Bible, the brain is mentioned only once, but the word "heart" is mentioned hundreds of times. The Bible clearly tells us that the real issues of our life should be spiritual and not material. Spiritually, when referring to the heart, it is about the inner person. The multiple use of the word "heart" as a suffix, describes a person inner self. For example to say someone is broken-hearted means someone's heart has been broken and they are burdened with great sorrow, grief, or disappointment.

During our lifetime we will encounter some very interesting, complicated, and complex individuals that will display the condition of their heart. Some people's hearts can be described as being: light-hearted, broken-hearted, tender-hearted, hard-hearted, good-hearted, true-hearted, black-hearted, whole-hearted, cold-hearted, big-hearted, half-hearted, soft-hearted, heavy-hearted, and the likes. What we say when speaking, and how we act in behavior, are all products of what we are on the inside. It's about the heart.

The heart is the source of our feelings, compassion, empathy, love, sexual desire, sorrow, adoration, disgust, satisfaction. Feelings are important because they are responsible for our entire experience of life. Our feelings motivate us to do things.

The heart is our control center for which all our decisions are made. Our heart controls our thoughts, attitudes, actions, beliefs, values, and convictions. The heart is the core of the type of person you are. Your heart is, YOU. Jesus said, "...It is the thoughtlife that pollutes. For from within, out of men's hearts, come evil thoughts of lust, theft, murder, adultery, wanting what belongs to others, wickedness, deceit, lewdness, envy, slander, pride, and all other folly. All theses vile things come from within; they are what pollute you and make you unfit for God" (Mark 7:20-23).

The Lord simply tells us that ALL sin is generated in the heart. The heart is connected to our mind, will, and understanding. The Bible warns us about the different types of hearts from a contrite heart to a willing heart. It talks about the heart not of God: obstinate heart, proud heart, wicked heart, fixed heart, perverse heart, diabolical heart, haughty heart, stoney heart, deceitful heart, mischievous heart. Then it describe a different type of heart: grieved heart, willing heart, trembling heart, perfect heart, soft heart, tender heart, pure heart, upright heart, sorrowful heart, true heart, compassionate heart.

God searches our hearts. God knows the secrets of our hearts. God gives us a solution for a sinful heart, Jesus Christ. Then God demands that we love Him with our whole heart, soul, mind, and strength. "Take delight in the Lord, and he will give you the desires of your heart. Commit your way to the Lord; trust in him and he will do this: He will make your righteous reward shine like the dawn, your vindication like the noonday sun" (Psalm 37:4-6).

You may be able to fool some people some of the time and some people all the time, but you can NEVER fool God, any time. Only God knows the true status of our heart. We may be able to fool a lot of people, but you can never fool God. What is the status of your heart? Only God can allow your heart to beat. Is your heart beating for God or against God?

HARD-HEARTED

What is the meaning of hard-hearted? The meaning of hard-hearted is someone who is hard-hearted, have or show no kindness or sympathy for other people. Proverbs 28:14 says, "How blessed is the man who fears always, But he who hardens his heart will fall into calamity." Proverbs 6:16-19 states, "For there are six things the Lord hates - no, seven: haughtiness, lying, murdering, plotting evil, eagerness to do wrong, a false witness, sowing discord among brothers."

What kind of person comes to mind when you think of a person with a hard-heart? A hard-hearted person is heartless, callous, indifferent, uncompassionate, and unemotional. They have no consideration for man, woman, nor beast. Do you think that I was just talking about the devil? Absolutely not! I am going to tell you something, people can have a hard-heart without those closest to them ever realizing it. I have known a lot of preachers standing in the church's pulpit that are hard-hearted. I have seen some of the most attractive women and men displaying the friendliest smile, but their hearts are hard.

The idea of hardening a heart is first found in the Bible in reference to Pharaoh. God told Moses, "When you arrive back in Egypt you are to go to Pharaoh and do the miracles I have shown you, but I will make him stubborn so that he will not let the people go. Then you are to tell him, 'Jehovah says, "Israel is my eldest son, and I have commanded you to let him go away and worship me, but you have refused: and now see, I will slay your eldest son"' "(Exodus 4:21-23). God told Moses that Pharaoh wouldn't listen, but this will give Him the opportunity to do some mighty miracles to demonstrate His power (Exodus 11:9).

Pharaoh resisted all efforts of Moses to release the children of Israel. Plague after plague, Pharaoh heart got harder and harder. Eventually, Pharaoh lost, he lost his son, and Egypt saw the devastation by the death angel, all because he was hard-hearted.

The saddest thing about a hard-hearted person, they don't know that they are heartless. Something has happened to them that made them brokenhearted. They trusted someone, that hurt, rejected, or betrayed them. Usually they will promise themselves that they will never allow themselves to be vulnerable again. Bitterness takes root and the hardness begins to set in. Their unhealed broken heart becomes hardened.

The heart encompasses our emotions, aspirations, and beliefs. Scripture tells us to, "Above all else, guard your heart, for it is the wellspring of life" (Proverbs 4:23). Jesus said, "A good man out of the good treasure of his heart brings forth good; and an evil man out of the evil treasure of his heart brings forth evil. For out of the abundance of the heart, his mouth speaks" (Luke 6:45).

People are hard-hearted because they chose to be. We make our choices and some times our choices makes us. If our hearts become hardened, we chose to harden them. And yet, there is still hope for hard-hearted people. Our God can change the hardest hearts, "I will give you a new heart and put a new spirit within you; I will take the heart of stone out of your flesh and give you a heart of flesh" (Ezekiel 36:26). I have seen God changed one of the hardest hearts I have ever known. Only God could have done this. I watched that person do a complete 180 degree, from a hard-heart to a soft-heart. I have also seen some soft-hearts turn to hard-hearts.

WINGS TO FLY AWAY

"Oh that I had wings like a dove for then I would I fly away and be at rest" (Psalm 55:6).

Absalom, David's third son, by Maacah, led a rebellion against David. King David was forced to leave his beloved Jerusalem in order for it not to be destroyed. As he left his city, he walked up the road that led to the Mount of Olives. He wept as he left. His head was covered and his feet were bare as a sign of mourning. Then someone told him that Ahithophel, a member of his cabinet, more importantly, one of David's most trusted advisers, and close friend, had betrayed him. Ahithophel had gone over to the side of Absalom (2 Samuel 15:13-32).

What a betrayal! David received a double betrayal, first his son, then his closest friend. Betrayal feels like someone have stabbed you in the back. Betrayal is a breach of trust and that trust you gave them, they decided that you were not worth keeping that trust. It is one of the most painful experiences in life. One of the worst kinds of pain.

Betrayal feels like a crushing blow to the head. From the first blow, you become dazed and confused. The saddest thing about betrayal, it never comes from your enemies. You only can be betrayed by someone you trust, like a friend, a family member, or a love one.

Listen to David description of his pain, "For it was not an enemy who reproaches and taunts me -- then I might bear it; nor is it one who has hated me who insolently vaunts himself against me -- then I might hide from him. But it was you, a man my equal, my companion and my familiar friend. We had sweet fellowship together and used to walk to the house of God in company" (Psalm 55:12-14).

Betrayal is not the only heartache we will experience in life that makes us want wings to fly away. There will be many difficult life situations that makes us want to take wings and fly away, or run and hide, steal away, head for the hills, fly the coop, hightail-it, take to the woods, and runaway; such as breakups, losing a job, failures, sickness, injuries, the loss of a love one.

Have you ever found yourself wishing you had wings to fly away to avoid that situation that is causing you so much pain? There have been a few, very painful situations in my life, that I wished I could have sprouted wings, to fly away from. But even if we could leave that situation behind us physically, in most cases, we couldn't leave it behind us, mentally.

Those wings that we seek to fly away on, instead of us wanting to literally run from life's troubles, we can place those problems on the wings of God, by turning them over to Him. Sometimes we forget that God has given us a Counselor, Helper, and Comforter, and He lives within us. He is the Holy Spirit who helps us, encourages us, comforts us, and strengthens us.

We all have circumstances that causes us duress. When you feel like flying away, or powerless, or tired, God is there with you and you are never alone. The Holy Spirit is there to help you. He is the Source that has the power to sustain you, energize you, and to renew you. He can take all of your problems and place them on wings, to fly away. Then He will place you on the wings of an eagle, refreshed, and with renewed strength. How do I know? He told us in Isaiah 40:29-31, "He gives power to the tired and worn out, and strength to the weak. Even the youths shall be exhausted, and the young men will all give up. But they that wait upon the Lord shall renew their strength. They shall mount up with wings like eagles; they shall run and not be weary; they shall walk and not faint."

We must remember that the Lord is always near us. We should never be anxious about anything. I know this is easier said than done, but it is true. Anxiousness is always an unwanted guest in our lives, but by trusting God in everything, you can always get your unwanted guest (anxious) out of your life. How? Go to God in prayer and leave your troubles there, then trust Him, rest in Him. He will provide you with His peace, that goes beyond our understanding. He promised to guard our minds and hearts. "Don't worry about anything; instead, pray about everything; tell God your needs and don't forget to thank him for his answers. If you do this you will experience God's peace, which is far more wonderful than the human mind can understand. His peace will keep your thoughts and your hearts quiet and at rest as you trust in Christ Jesus" (Philippians 4:6-7).

MERCY'S DOOR

What is mercy? The dictionary defines mercy as the compassionate treatment of those in distress, especially when it is within one's power to punish them.

The word "mercy" derives from the Latin merced or merces. It means "price paid." Mercy appears in the Bible as forgiveness or withholding punishment. God's mercy means His pity, compassion, and kindness toward people. Mercy is forgiveness. Mercy is forgiving the sinner and withholding the punishment that is justly deserved.

The word "door" is used in the Bible over 400 times as a metaphor for opportunities in our lives. Doors are usually thresholds in which we cross over from one kind of place to another. Doors are used as exits and entrances. A door is like a portal, it can leave to almost anything, like a new beginning, a challenge, or an opportunity. A close door can represent a dead end with feelings of no way out or someone is blocking you. There are the revolving doors, like you are moving in circles and not going anywhere. There are times when a door may be slammed in your face. There you feel shut out and ignored.

When God opens a door no one can close it. God is our Doorkeeper! God is sovereign. He is in complete control. God is all-knowing (omniscient) and all-powerful (omnipotent). He knows everything we have done and what we will do, both the good and the bad. "I know you well; you aren't strong, but you have tried to obey and have not denied my Name. Therefore I have opened a door to you that no one can shut" (Revelation 3:8).

Do you know that God has many doors opened for you? One such door is called the Mercy Door. It is an open door that will always remain open. There at the Mercy Door of God is forgiveness. "If we confess our sins, He is faithful and righteous to forgive us our sins and to cleanse us from all unrighteousness" (1 John 1:9). Forgiveness is choosing not to hold an offense against someone. Forgiveness is choosing not to keep records nor dwell on the offense. That is what God did for us. How? Through the death and resurrection of Jesus, our sins is no longer counted against us. Our sin made us guilty, but the guilty receives forgiveness instead of punishment.

There at the Mercy Door of God is compassion. "The Lord is compassionate and gracious, slow to anger, abounding in love" (Psalm 103:8). Compassion is feeling sympathy or pity for others. God has given us a powerful promise of compassion. His compassion is not the result of what we do, but because of His boundless love for us.

There at the Mercy Door of God is gentleness. "But the wisdom from above is first pure, then peaceable, gentle, open to reason, full of mercy and good fruits, impartial and sincere" (James 3:17). Gentleness is the quality of being kind, tender, mildness of temper, sweetness of disposition. God is gentle and He has always been gentle towards us, even in correcting us.

There at the Mercy Door of God is love. "For I am convinced that nothing can ever separate us from his love. Death can't, and life can't. The angels won't, and all the powers of hell itself cannot keep God's love away. Our fears for today, our worries about tomorrow, or where we are - high above the sky, or in the deepest ocean - nothing will ever be able to separate us from the love of God demonstrated by our Lord Jesus Christ when he died for us" (Romans 8:38-39).

We are an underserving recipient of God's mercy. "The Lord, the Lord, a God, merciful and gracious, slow to anger, and abounding in steadfast love and faithfulness, keeping steadfast love for thousands, forgiving iniquity and transgression and sin, but who will by no means clear the guilty, visiting the iniquity of the fathers on the children and the children's children, to the third and the fourth generation" (Exodus 34:6-7). God gives us His loving mercy. His mercy means His pity, forgiveness, compassion, gentleness, generosity, sympathy, goodwill, love, kindness and so much more. God's mercy tells us who He is, His gentleness, His forgiveness, His endless love for us. Because of our sin nature, we don't deserve His mercy. God displays His goodness through His grace and mercy. God loves us and He spills out His mercy on us as His act of love. God mercy is tender, great, everlasting, manifested, exemplified, sure, plenteous, abundant, and He is rich in His mercy, as He reigns high in heaven while sitting on His mercy-seat. Praise God! Hallelujah!

NEVERTHELESS

Nevertheless means, in spite of. Nevertheless is an underused word and its power is underestimated. Nevertheless, places all the power into the hands of God. With this one word, we can change the course of our entire life. The word "nevertheless" appears in the bible over 200 times.

Paul was sent to Rome as a prisoner to make his appeal to Caesar. He was placed on a ship, along with some other prisoners. The ship was scheduled to make several stops along the Turkish coast. They made a temporary stop at Sidon and when they left Sidon, they encountered some strong winds that made it difficult to keep the ship on course. Paul spoke to the ship's officers and warned them there will be trouble ahead. "Nevertheless," the officers in charge of the prisoners listened to the ship's captain instead of taking heed to Paul's warning. So they set sail and suddenly the weather changed. They were out in the Mediterranean Sea being driven westward from the island of Crete. It looked like they would wreck on the island of Claudia. They had to let the wind take the ship. They threw all the cargo overboard to lighten the ship's load.

After fourteen days of wind and waves, they felt this was it. They wouldn't come out of this storm alive. However, an angel of the Lord had appeared to Paul and said, "...Don't be afraid, Paul - for you will surely stand trial before Caesar. What's more, God has granted your request and will save the lives of all those sailing with you" (Acts 27:24). Paul proceeded to tell them to keep up their courage, because he had faith in God and things will happen just as God told him. "Nevertheless, we must run aground on some island" (Acts 27:26). Nevertheless, Paul was determined to believe the faithfulness of God, the promises of God, and God proved Himself to be faithful.

The power of "nevertheless" can change any situation or problem from a negative one, to a positive one. There are so many more biblical examples of how the Power of "NEVERTHELESS" has been harnessed:

> Abraham would say, "When I had to leave my homeland and didn't know where to go, but nevertheless."
>
> Daniel said, "Nevertheless I will read the writing to the king, and make known the interpretation."
>
> Noah would say, "When no one would listen to me, but nevertheless."

Nehemiah said, "Nevertheless in your manifold mercies you did not make a full end of them, nor forsake them; for you are a gracious and merciful God."

Jeremiah would say, "When my own family turned against me, but nevertheless."

Deborah said, "I will surely go with you: nevertheless, the journey that you take shall not be for your honor."

Jonah would say, "When I don't want to do it, but nevertheless."

Job said, "I have no hope. 'Nevertheless,' I will maintain my ways before him."

Joseph would say, "When I was mistreated and wrongly accused, but nevertheless."

Joshua said, "Nevertheless, my brothers who went up with me made the heart of the people melt; but I wholly followed the LORD my God."

David would say, "When everything goes against common sense and I was running for my life, but nevertheless."

Jesus said, "Father, if you are willing, remove this cup from me. Nevertheless, not my will but yours, be done." AND "Nevertheless, I tell you, after this you will see the Son of Man sitting at the right hand of Power, and coming on the clouds of the sky."

So how would you apply the power of "Nevertheless" in your life? If your marriage is not working out the way you planned it, but "nevertheless" - I will trust God with my future. If your health is not improving although you have constantly fasted and prayed about it, but "nevertheless" - I will serve God with all my heart and soul. Maybe you are all alone and lonely, but "nevertheless" - you are never alone because Jesus is always with you. Maybe someone has really hurt you badly, but "nevertheless" - God will give you forgiving power and vengeance belongs to the Lord. Your life has turned out disastrously, but "nevertheless" - your future is secure and is being orchestrated by Jesus. Maybe you are in the midst of a crisis, " nevertheless" - God has all power in His hands and nothing is impossible with God.

The power of "nevertheless" can change anything and everything. The Power of "nevertheless" simply means that you have placed **ALL** of your trust in the Lord, but "nevertheless" if He doesn't do what you desire of Him, it was not in His will for you. God is a God that we can always count on. He is a God that you can always trust.

God always want what is best for us. He is always on our side. He is worthy of all our trust. He has proven Himself to us, over and over again. God always wants to help you. Trusting in God is a matter of your personal faith. When you are afraid, put your trust in God. In times of adversity, trust in God at all times, because operating by faith in the face of adversity is a Fruit of the Spirit.

No matter what you are going through, what you are dealing with, what oppositions you are facing, in order to have peace, you will need to develop a "nevertheless" attitude about it in order to receive the peace of Jesus. In other words, "nevertheless" is all about completely trusting God. It's about letting go, and letting God. There will come a point in your life where you have to make a decision whether you are going to trust God, or man, or yourself. If God brings you to it, He can bring you through it. Believe me, that "nevertheless" moment, issue, or situation, is not to harm you, but to make you better. No matter what, trust God. Only God can take what you think is a negative "nevertheless" and turn it into a positive one.

POTHOLES OF LIFE

Potholes are holes in the roadway that vary in size and shape. They are caused by the expansion and contraction of ground water after the water has entered into the ground under the pavement.

Lately, our local news network has been featuring stories about the potholes in our city's roads, and the damage they cause on vehicles. The other day I had to run an errand. I was in an unfamiliar area. I was so focused on trying to locate a particular business that I wasn't watching the road, itself. So, I didn't see the pothole, and my car hit a huge one. I felt the thump, and I definitely heard it as it scraped my left rim.

As we journey through the road of life, we will experience many potholes. The potholes are unavoidable and inevitable. These potholes will manifest itself whenever it pleases, wrecking havoc in our life. They come in all shapes and sizes. From miniature, to the giant size like Goliath. Just like a human being, a pothole has a beginning and it has an ending. Unlike human beings, it has no parents, but they have relatives, like affliction, hardship, distress, adversity, and so on. There will be potholes that will negatively affect you. Deep in its cavity you will find grief, heartache, misery, and misfortune. Just when you think you have cleared all the potholes, out of nowhere, you will hit a bump in the road full of trouble, problems, challenges and difficulties. There are no ways to skip over them, to avoid them and no ways to go around them.

The Bible tells us that all things work together for good to them that love God, to them who are the called according to his purpose" (Romans 8:28). But we often wonder, why does bad things always happen to good people? We have to learn, and the only way to learn is through experience. We need to view "bad things" as "good things in disguise." WHAT? Yes! Our God is Sovereign. Nothing can happen to us unless He allows it to happen. If He has allowed it, that means that He wants His children to develop into our spiritual maturity.

You see, when you accepted Jesus Christ as your Savior, a supernatural work began transforming you into the image of Christ. To mature your faith, God will use trials and tests to develop your character. Through the grace of God, when you respond to those trials and tests, you experience the power of God's Spirit, which manifest in your life through the Fruit of the Spirit: love, joy, peace, long-suffering, gentleness, goodness, faith, meekness, and self-control (see Galatians 5:22-23).

Scripture says, "Beloved, think it not strange concerning the fiery trial which is to try you, as though some strange thing happened unto you: but rejoice, inasmuch as ye are partakers of Christ's sufferings; that, when his glory shall be revealed, ye may be glad also with exceeding joy" (1 Peter 4:12-13).

Every child of God will probably have to face many tests. These are just a few examples:

* Fiery Trials: Intense encounters or struggles; bursts of anger, grief, or lust.

* Temptations: Opportunities to yield to our sinful nature.

* Distress: Disappointments and deep hurts.

* Infirmities: Physical limitations and illnesses.

* Tribulations: Unusual pressures and challenges.

* Persecutions: Harassment and oppression due to religious convictions.

* Necessities: Wear and care of daily responsibilities.

* Reproaches: Ridicule and rejection on account of faith or holiness.

As I said earlier, God will not allow anything to happen to you without His permission. Our trials and tests are opportunities to grow spiritually. We must choose to trust God and accept the grace that He gives us, and Christ's character will be formed within us. Trials produce maturity. "We glory in tribulations also: knowing that tribulation worketh patience; and patience, experience; and experience, hope: and hope maketh not ashamed;

because the love of God is shed abroad in our hearts by the Holy Ghost which is given unto us (Romans 5:3-5).

Believe it or not, the trials and tests in our life are for our good. You can be assured the trials are in accordance to God's will in our life. They are part of His perfect plan for us. God will give you everything you will need to get through those trials and tests, victoriously. They are meant to make you into the person God wants you to be. One day you will look back and see the growth from those trials and test.

"IT"

In grammar, "IT" is a pronoun. We commonly use the pronoun "it" as both a subject and an object pronoun. "It" can be used as the subject, object, or compliment of a verb or the object of a preposition. "It" is used to refer to a thing previously mentioned or easily identified ("a room with two beds in it"). "It" can be used to identify a person ("it's me").

In our life's journey, there will be some highs and lows, some ups and downs, some good and bad, some happiness and sadness, some bitterness and sweetness. It appears that the good times in life is so short lived and the bad times lingers on far too long. Disappointments sashays in our lives like an unwanted guest. We are disappointed by life situations, things, people, and events.

"It" could be a health issue. There comes a time in our life when we are not as healthy as we used to be. It could be something major and something minor. Sometimes when a health issue occurs, we have the tendency to dismiss it or ignore it, pretending that "it" will go away or "it" doesn't exist. Either way, "it" really does exist, rather "it" is minor or major.

"It" could be a workplace problem. The workplace is suppose to be the place where you go in and fulfill your professional obligation that you were hired to do, but we all know that you will face many issues and problems that will blindside you. Things happen that you never expected, thereby causing you to become surprise and frustrated. Sometimes the issues and problems can be resolved quickly and sometimes not. "It" really is real.

"It" could be a friendship issue. We need friends in our life. We share our life together with our friends. We share our sorrows with our friends. We share our thoughts with our friends. We even share our happiness with our friends. But sometimes our relationship with our friends can cause us some trouble. Things can ruin a friendship, like jealousy, betrayal, backstabbing, and lies. How can you start out being such good friends and then the relationship turns toxic? "It" really does happen.

"It" could be a financial crisis. Life has its uncertainties. You can have "it" going on one day and by the next day, the bottom falls out. A financial crisis can happen at any stage of our life. No matter how you think you have prepared for your financial uncertainties, a financial crisis can catch you totally off-guard. Especially from the result of lingering unemployment and a constant decline in your investment portfolio, or your business takes a major financial hit. "It" can be really costly.

"It" is the operative word. "It" could be a wondering spouse, a disobedient child, an unequally yoke relationship, or being underemployed or unemployed. "It" could be some type of career pressure, unfair treatment, inner peace, a mental health issue, and the list can go on and on. "It" could be anything that disturbs your peace and sense of well being.

I have some good news for you concerning, "IT." Whatever "IT" is, God can handle "IT." Did you know that the word "it" appears over 5,000 times in the King James version of the Bible? God isn't expecting you to handle everything. Some things He wants you to give to Him. Now, please don't get me wrong. There are some things that happens that God did not cause, but He allowed "it" to happen. And sometimes He allows more and more things to happen. Thus, "...My son don't be angry when the Lord punished you. Don't be discouraged when he has to show you where you are wrong. For when he punishes you, it proves that he loves you. When he whips you it proves you are really his child" (Hebrews 12:5b-7). Sometimes this becomes a great benefit for our character and our walk, because "it" becomes a great life lesson. We end up learning a great lesson, instead of receiving the victory in a particular situation.

There are somethings that you can't handle and those things you must give them to God. He does give us plenty of things that we can't handle on our own. "It" is not meant for us to handle on our own, because we are not self-sufficient. We can't do nothing on our own. When Jesus walked this dusty earth, he once said, "I can of myself do nothing" (John 5:30). Some battles are not ours to fight. In some cases, God tells us, "You will not need to fight in this battle. Position yourselves, stand still and see the salvation of the Lord, who is with you" (2 Chronicles 20:17). We can't understand what's going on and why it is going on. We must always trust God and His purpose for our life. God will always prompt you when to move and when to be still. There will be times when you will be placed in a situation where you can't hide from your problem. You can't ignore the problem. You can't run from the problem. You must face the "it", endure "it", learn from "it", and grow from "it." In other words, you can't do nothing, but give "it" to God and let Him handle "it." Amen!

UNRAVELING

Unravel is defined as to solve, untangle or undo, or to become untangled. What is emotional unraveling? Emotional unraveling often involves a fierce emotion that overwhelms people. Simply put, it means to fall apart emotionally. Can a person really unravel? The psychological state of unraveling can happen to anyone, given the nature and degree of stress lying beyond someone's personal endurance.

There is only so much emotional stress a person can handle. You think that you are ravel, but ravel is the same as unravel, both words are synonyms and antonyms. Ravel means tangled or untangled. Just like a loose thread in a knitted cap or sweater, raveling could lead to more unraveling, where it looks like you can no longer tell up from down nor left from right. You become like a lost ship at sea and you are in the midst of a storm. You feel like a broken down car, totally immobile. You feel discombobulated. What a horrible feeling! Depending on your degree of stress, the unraveling can happen to anyone of us, on any given day, at any given moment. Only God knows how much you can endure, and any negative changes in our personal life can trigger unbelievable stress, from the loss of a loved one, financial problems, marital problems, mental and physical abuse, job loss, illness, etc. "The Lord is good, a stronghold in the day of trouble; he knows those who take refuge in him" (Nahum 1:7).

When I look in the rearview mirror of my memories, there was a point in my life that I felt like an unraveled ball of yarn. I was not at the point of full unravel, but I was right at that door. I could see the trail of string unwinding ever so slowly and becoming longer and longer. I was standing at the cliff of a mountain, the slightest wind could have pushed me over the edge. The yarn in my life had made a perfect knitted sweater of protection for me. But the yarn was unraveling from the sweater and so was my level of protection from it.

When I revisit those memories, I understand that I couldn't go back in time to fix anything. I can only relive it and revisit it, and I feel that crippling pain that comes by the visitation of that experience. I was almost a train wreck ready to happen. I was wearing a figurative sign flashing the words of, "I am a Hot Mess and I am on a train whose name is The Hot Mess Express." All of my feelings flowed, starting from the engine, all the way back to the caboose. It's like being at a train station and you hear the words, "All Abroad," and that represents everything that means unravel.

Showers of Blessings

While on "The Hot Mess Express," all of my unraveling components of emotions had chained themselves to me emotionally, and filled every inch of me psychologically.

On "The Hot Mess Express," the baggage car was tagged, "troubled souls" only. The carriage of the train was labeled "Dysfunction Junction." Each compartment car was filled with depression and was shouting, "This lady is singing the blues." The dining car restaurant's lights was so dimmed that you could see the shadows of detached emotions. The buffet table was serving a bitter delicacy listing numerous kinds of emotional pains. The engine wasn't just pulling the train and it's cars, but it was also pulling a huge container, oozing with disconnection and detached feelings. The luggage racks were storing bags filled with disentangled thoughts. From the observation car, the only view available was clouds displaying worry and anxiety. The corridor of the train was lined with wallpaper containing high stress levels, which was extremely potent. The train was pulling a flatcar carrying loads of anguish and depression. In the quiet carriage, passengers were asked not to use their cell phones, but you would never believe what happened. Emotional exhaustion kept sending me texts on my cell phone, about my physical exhaustion. Imagine that! I was on the verge of a breakdown.

Slowly the threads of my life was unraveling. I didn't see it at first, but as the threads of my life slowly started to unravel, from hindsight, I was a "Hot Mess" traveling down the emotional distress train tracks on "The Hot Mess Express." Prayer, winded up the unraveled ball of yarn, and God reached down and grab me. "Likewise the Spirit helps us in our weakness. For we do not know what to pray for as we ought, but the Sprit himself intercedes for us with groanings too deep for words" (Romans 8:26). Then GOD wrapped His long arms of protection around me and said, "Not on my watch." I thank God for rescuing me. I am also thankful that He reminds me that by His stripes we are healed. Faith unlocks any door to the power of God. What a revelation! This revelation unraveled me, in a good way. Only God could wind that ball of yarn up again. I can now unravel all the weights that were easily besetting me. God reminded me that, "He created my inmost being; He knitted me together in my mothers womb." What God create and knit together does not unravel. God's Word was my lifeline. My prayers to God was my lifeline. Although I couldn't see Him, I could hear and feel Him. God is near to us even in our darkest moments.

If you have ever felt this way, you truly understand what this feels like. If you are feeling fragile, it is not okay. God reminds us, "Come to me, all who labor and are heavy laden, and I will give you rest. Take my yoke upon you, and learn from me, for I am gentle and lowly in heart, and you will find rest for your souls. For my yoke is easy, and my burden is light" (Matthew 11:28-30).

Stop minimizing and trivializing your pain. If you need help, please get help! Trust me, you are not alone. You are worth the effort to fight for yourself. God knitted you together and what He knits together shall not unravel.

"For I know the plans I have for you, declares the Lord, plans for welfare and not for evil, to give you a future and a hope. Then you will call upon me and come and pray to me, and I will hear you. You will seek me and find me, when you seek me with all your heart" (Jeremiah 29:11-13).

HERO!

How would you define a hero? A hero is a real person or a main fictional character who, in facing danger, combats adversity through feat of ingenuity, courage, or strength. Qualities of a hero includes, but not limited to, loyalty, compassion, sacrifice, bravery, conviction, courage, determination, helpful, honesty, inspirational, moral integrity, dedication, valor, selfless, perseverance, and fortitude.

Movies are always telling stories about heroes. Some are non-fictional and some are fictional stories such as Batman, Superman, Wonder Woman, Superwoman, Spider Man, Iron Man, Thor, Cinderella, Maleficent, Black Swan, Hansel & Gretel, Snow White, etc.

Heroes have empathy toward others and understand other people's perspective. Heroes are concern for the well-being of others. Heroes have very special skills and displays much strength. Heroes are extremely competent and very confident (most times). Heroes have strong moral characters. Heroes understand and knows that there is a fear factor involved at times and yet they are not afraid to face them.

The Bible tells us about some real life heroes and there are so many of them. Abraham was a hero in the Bible. At the age of 75, God directed him to leave the land of his people and family to go to a foreign land. He married Sarah and she was infertile, although God promised him that he would be the father of a great nation. God told him that his offspring would be as the stars in the sky, he wouldn't be able to count them. He believed the promises of God and God called him His friend. When Abraham was 100 years old, his son Isaac was born. Abraham absolutely trusted God by faith.

Esther and Mordecai were heroes in the Bible. Esther was an orphan, adopted and raised by her cousin Mordecai. Esther was chosen for King Ahasuerus, the king of Persia, because of her beauty and intelligence. King Ahasuerus was so pleased with her that he crowned her as his queen. Mordecai had a enemy and his name was Haman. Haman hated Mordecai so much that he had the king to sign a decree to killed all the Jews in the Persia Empire. It was the love of their people that saved the Jews of Persia from genocide.

David was a hero in the Bible. When he was a young boy he was a shepherd. He was strong and brave, he killed a lion, a bear, and a giant. He was anointed to be king of Israel at a young age. He had to constantly run for his life, because King Saul wanted to kill him, but David never lifted a hand to harm King Saul in anyway. Later when David became king, he had to flee his throne, because his son Absalom wanted to kill him. In David's adult life, he sinned, he murdered, he confessed his sins, and he wept over them. God said that David was a man after His own heart.

I would like to introduce you the greatest Hero of all times. He is not just a Hero, but a Superhero. He is the Bread from Heaven and the Bread of Life. He is the Heir of all things. He is our High Priest. He is the Holy and Righteous One. He is the Lamb of God and the Light of the World. He is the Tribe of Judah and Lord of all. He is the Lord or lords, King of kings, and God of gods. He is the Bright and Morning Star. He is the Perfecter of our faith and Prince of Peace. He is the Resurrection and the Life. He is the Ruler of God's Creation. He is the Way, the Truth, and the Life. He is Alpha and Omega, the beginning and the end. WOW!

The entire Bible is all about Him. The Old Testament talks about the coming King and the New Testament tells us about this King's life, death, resurrection, and His second coming. He is the Living Word. "In the beginning was the Word, and the Word was with God, and the Word was God. He was with God in the beginning. Through him all things were made; without him nothing was made that has been made. In him was life, and that life was the light of men. The light shines in the darkness, but the darkness has not understood it" (John 1:1-5). Isn't this mind-blowing?

"The Word became flesh and made his dwelling among us. We have seen his glory, the glory of the One and Only, who came from the Father, full of grace and truth" (John 1:14). DROP THE MIC! Not only was Christ there in the beginning, He came down from His regal throne in heaven, took the form of a human baby, grew up like we all did. He wasn't even born into a wealthy family.

"He had no beauty or majesty to attract us to him, nothing in his appearance that we should desire him." He grew up to be a man and He never sinned. Awesome!

He didn't have a medical degree, but He is the Best Healer the world has ever had and will ever have. He never took a psychology class, yet He is a Mighty Counselor and He can help you with any mental or emotional trauma. He has more followers than all of FaceBook, Twitter, and Instagram, together. Oooh wee!

"For in Christ all the fullness of the Deity lives in bodily form, and you have been given fullness in Christ, who is the head over every power and authority" (Colossians 2:9). Him and the Father are One. There is only one God, but He exists in three persons, God the Father, God the Son, and God the Holy Spirit. The Father is God, the Son is God, and the Holy Spirit is God. The Father is not the same person as the Son, nor is the Son the same person as the Holy Spirit.

The greatest Hero of all times and forevermore shall be, is JESUS CHRIST! He came to earth as a baby then grew to be a man. Totally sinless! He healed, he taught, he corrected, he led, he fed, he died, and he rose from the dead. There He sits in heaven on the right hand side, on the throne with our Father. He is a heart changer, a mind regulator, our Protector, our Provider, our Sustainer, our Savior, our Redeemer, and our Friend. Despite of our sins, He loves us totally unconditionally. He makes intercessions for us, to the Father. He has prepared a place for us in heaven. He is the greatest of all times! My Hero. Our Hero. What a HERO! No. HE IS A **SUPERHERO**!

VILLAIN?

Villains are real people that plots, to somehow cause harm or ruin to someone or something. They can be anyone with varying social and economic backgrounds. A Villain could be a politician, a religious leader, teacher, student, family member, or anyone.

Did you know that there are different types of Villains? Of yes there are! There are so many types of Villains. The types of Villains are as follows:

1) Traitor - This villain betrays the ones who trusted him or her.
2) Patriarch or Matriarch - This villain operates as the head of the family or group.

3) Tyrant - This villain doesn't take no stuff from anybody. You do as you are told or suffer the consequences.
4) Outcast - This villain is shunned or in exiled from the family or community and seeks getting revenge.
5) Evil genus - This villain is highly intelligent and sees himself or herself as superior to others.
6) Schemer - This villain loves developing diabolical plans and have the capacity to carry them out.
7) Lunatic - This villain is just plain crazy. They may not have any real motivation or legitimacy for their crazy conspiracies.
8) Fanatic - This villain have some very strong beliefs and their beliefs will take them to the max, because they really believe that what they are doing is for the best.
9) Devil - The Devil, also known as Satan. He is the chief of the Villains. He is the personification of evil. He is called many different names in various cultures:

Beelzebub, Lucifer, Satan, Apollyon, Antichrist, demon, and Mephistopheles, just to name a few. This malevolent being and his legion of demons continues to strike fear in people and wreck havoc in people's lives. He is the enemy of God and those who seek to do the will of our Heavenly Father.

In the movies and in any work of literature, the villain plays an important role in the story, because without the villain, we really can't see how good the hero is. We wouldn't be able to see nor understand the dangers that a person or a community is facing.

Guess what? We wouldn't have no one to hate or blame for all of the problems and chaos that was caused. The bad ways of the villain displays the goodness of the hero.

There are all kinds of fictional villains. Some of my favorites villains are:

1) Freddy Krueger - He played a villain in The Nightmare on Elm Street.
2) Michael Myers - He played the villain in The Halloween Series.
3) Hannibal Lector - He played the villain in The Silence of The Lambs, Hannibal, and Red Dragon.
4) The Joker - He played the villain in Batman, Dark Knight, and Joker.
5) Darth Vader - He played the villain in Star Wars

Hey, guess what I just noticed, I didn't include any females villains. I wonder why? Maybe I only identity with the real ones that have cross my path in my REAL life. Funny, haha! But it's true. Praise God for His Word, because the Bible says, "Don't do as the wicked do. Avoid their haunts - turn away, go somewhere else, for evil men can't sleep until they've done their evil deed for the day. They can't rest unless they cause someone to stumble and fall. They eat and drink wickedness and violence! But the good man walks along in the ever-brightening light of God's favor, the dawn gives way to morning splendor, while the evil man gropes and stumbles in the dark" (Proverbs 4:14-19).

There are some real life villains. We all have had an encounter with a villain, someway, somehow. Maybe from a co-worker, boss, ex-spouse, boyfriend, girlfriend, a so-called friend, family member, neighbor, church member, or anyone that tries to make your life misery, just because they can.

During our lifetime, whether we like it or not, we are going to run into someone who will affect us in some way or another. Sometimes they will affect us in a positive way and sometimes in a negative way. So far in my life, there has been more negative than positive experiences. Those negative people will bring their "A" game for a full negative attack against you and trust me, in most times unprovoked. Oftentimes you are totally blind-sided, leaving you traumatized and devastated. In storytelling, this attacker would definitely be considered, not just a villain, but the "best kind of Villain."

People often allow these Villains in their life, to become the reason why some things don't work for them. They begin to think that maybe they were the reason they became stuck-in-neutral and they can't move forward in their life. They start thinking that someone had done them wrong and they just can't get over it. They truly believe that so-in-so held them back from reaching their goals and potential, and that person shattered their dreams.

You didn't even realize that you were making those people Villains, and thereby making yourself a Victim. I have read that when someone gets fed up with being in the Victim Stage, the victim will start planning actions that can hurt others. That's when the Villain is born. A Villain will usually take revenge. A villain can become violent. A villain can become aggressive. A villain wants "pay back" for the sufferings that they have gone through. Sometimes you can become a villain without realizing that you are now the villain.

We all at one time in our life have been a Villain. If you are constantly criticizing someone, you are a Villain. If you are constantly calling someone out of their name, you are a Villain. If you are always putting someone down, you are a Villain. If you slander people, you are a Villain. If you are a gossiper, you are a Villain. If you are a constant liar, you are a Villain. Because what you are doing is EVIL. People do all kinds of immoral things to people and oftentimes, they want to play the role of the Victim, while all along they are truly the Villain.

Throughout Scripture, we are told to love others. We are not to hurt anyone, physically or mentally. But words really do hurt people. We should treat people the way we want to be treated, "Do unto others as you would have them do unto you" (Luke 6:31). Even if someone hurt you (and trust me, you will be hurt by someone), we are NOT suppose to, "do unto others the way others do us." Nor are we to, "do unto others before they do it to us."

We as Christians should always be imitators of Christ. We must be considerate of others. We must control what's in our hearts and what comes out of our mouths. Whenever you act out or react to a bad situation, once you say it or do it, you cannot take it back. You can be forgiven for the dirty deed, but trust me, it will not be forgotten. The tongue has no bones, but it's a mighty powerful weapon. It is strong enough to completely destroy a person and it can also break hearts.

Remember, "For we must all stand before Christ to be judged and have our lives laid bare - before him. Each of us will receive whatever he deserves for the good or bad things he has done in his earthly body" (2 Corinthians 4:10).

VICTIM?

We play many roles in our lives and in the lives of others. There are two major roles that we will see in any Hollywood movie that you may find on Amazon Prime, Netflix, HBO, HULU or wherever you watch your movies. In just about every movie there will be a victim, a villain, and most times a hero.

There are people that are true victims that have been victimized by real villains, through tragic crimes like rape and abuse (mental and/or physical). Sometimes you get caught-up by being in the wrong place at the wrong time and you become a victim. As a result, you suffer from some type of traumatic event. It doesn't matter the size of the event, whether large or small, it was traumatic to you and it caused a perpetual emotional cycle to you, the victim.

For anyone who has undergone a real traumatic event, they have to undergo the process of healing and this process isn't easy. For the real victims, I pray that your healing journey will bring about a self-awareness. This self-awareness will allow you to see yourself beyond the role of a victim. From self-awareness should birth self-compassion. From self-compassion you will realize that that you have been healed and that you are no longer a victim, but now you are a hero.

But sometimes we can be our own worst enemy. Some people can create the most creative crises, because they love to portray themselves as a victim. It's like there is a world-wide movement going on and this movement has a name. What is its name? The "Woe Is Me Movement!" Some people must be part of this movement by any means necessary. When you are part of this movement, it is easy to blame the world, find people to project hurt on, or create a toxic environment or situation to reduce your internal pain. With their delusions and compulsions, they don't realize that they have fallen into the vicious cycle of shame, blame, and denial.

Satan is the father of all lies and he wants every Believer to think that other people is causing bad things to happen to them and in their lives. He wants to capture your mind and keep you constantly upset, unforgiving, and bitter. He wants you to think that you will never catch a break. He wants you to think that bad things is always happening to you. He wants you to always feel sorry for yourself. He wants you to feel that you will always be a victim. He wants you to believe his lies.

Wait a minute! God understands it all. The Bible says that rain falls on the just as well as the unjust. God doesn't want you to have a mindset of a victim. God wants you to be free from any anger, malice, bitterness, and revenge. God wants you to have a mindset of an overcomer. He wants you to believe that, "I can do all things through Christ who strengthens me." He wants you to be more than a conqueror through Christ.

Yes, stuff happens in life. Our journey in this life will never be easy, because it will be a life full of hills and valleys. Jesus made us many promises, but He never promised us a problem free life. So, your husband, wife, boyfriend or girlfriend left you. So, you lost your job. So, you were overlooked for a promotion by someone who was less qualified than you. So, you loss a loved one. That's life! Please forgive me and I am not being insensitive, because each one of those scenarios have happened to me.

Jesus knows all about being a Victim. He is our Supreme example. He was victimized and He never developed a victim mentality. They spat on Him. They offered Him vinegar to drink. They mocked Him. They put a crown of thorns on His head. They hung Him on an old rugged cross. They did so much more and Jesus was completely innocent. There was no deceit found in Him, no guile, no sin of any kind! If anyone had a right to be a Victim, it was Jesus. "He never sinned, never told a lie, never answered back when insulted; when he suffered he did not threaten to get even; he left his case in the hands of God who always judges fairly" (1 Peter 2:22-23)

Okay, you got hurt. You are emotionally wounded. You have grieved, or now you are heavily grieving. There is a balm in Gilead. This balm is Jesus. By His stripes we are healed. He has the healing power that you need. He can wipe away your tears. Take your wounded, broken spirit to Jesus and tell Him all about. He already knows about it anyway. He is waiting on you.

ANGUISH

What is anguish? Anguish is often referred to as an emotional distress and can encompass a number of different emotions, such as trauma, grief, sorrow, fear, and anxiety. Anguish is one of the most painful emotions that can be felt by humans.

When the Amalekites raided David's camp at Ziklag, burned it, and took the women and children as captives, David was in deep (anguish) distress (1 Samuel 30). Hannah knows all about anguish. She wept and would not eat when they were making their annual trip to Shiloh, because she was deeply distressed (anguish) and she prayed to the Lord and wept bitterly (1 Samuel 1:7-10). Before Jesus' arrest, He went to Gethsemane to pray. In this moment we see Jesus in great emotional distress, "He took Peter and Zebedee's two sons, James and John, and He became anguished and distressed. He told them, 'My soul is crushed with grief to the point of death. Stay here and keep watch with me'" (Matthew 26:37-38).

The feeling of suffering from anguish is typically preceded by a tragedy or some kind of event that have a profound impact on that person. It is one of those feelings that hurts so deeply that there are no words to describe it. Someone may experience anguish through the loss of a loved one, divorce, or the termination of a long term relationship.

Anguish delivers an immense emotional complexity, and that is why so many people have difficulty coping with it. Anguish has the potential to change you. It can affect your motivation and attitude. How? One of the areas that mental anguish attacks is the brain. That heartbreak pain doesn't originate from the head, but from the brain. The brain is being attacked.

When I lost my husband, I was in severe pain and his loss affected me mentally and physically. The grief wrecked havoc on my well-being. I cannot begin to explain the pain, emptiness, and loss of someone that I LOVED, and had been with all of my adult life. His death was an extreme traumatic event in my life, and my anguish has lasted a very long time. I felt like someone had "stabbed me in the heart." I felt that I was dying on the inside.

My grief still remains, but not so intense. The wound is still there, but it is no longer so raw. This pain may never go away. I cannot disown my grief. I own it. All of it. We loved each other very hard, so my grief should be hard. He was worth my loving him; therefore, he is worth me grieving over him. This is my testimony of my love for him and his worth to me.

Mental anguish usually leads to depression. When you are depressed, you lose the desire to do anything or most things. If your depression is prolonged and left untreated, it could spiral out of control and result in a variety of many different problems. I know someone who lost their loved one, that person was so depressed that they were unable to work. Since they couldn't work, they lost their job, which affected their livelihood. They couldn't pay their mortgage nor any bills, which brought about more problems. Those problems kept stacking up on top of each other, which intensified her anguish.

Anguish affects your attitude. Even the most positive person's attitude can shift when followed by a tragedy. Sometimes, people will blame themselves for the tragedy. They will push other people away. Most of the time they want to be alone, because they don't desire any kind of social interaction.

If you or anyone you know is suffering from some type of mental anguish, please get some help. Believe me, you are not alone. Also know that the Bible addresses every type of issue that we will face in life, including anguish. The Bible helps us understand our emotions and how to express our emotions. The Bible is a very powerful tool, and we can use it to help navigate our pain and suffering. The Bible tells us that Christ is our hope in life and death. The Bible is the created spoken Word from God for our hearing and healing. We can take all of our problems to God through Jesus Christ. God knows everything about us and He knows when we are facing difficult times. Only God can give you the perfect guidance, comfort, and peace when you are heavy hearted. Whatever you are facing, take that situation to God. Nothing is too big for Him, be it a financial burden, a relationship problem, pain and suffering, joblessness, rejection, or grief. Give it to God.

Only God can help you in your times of anguish. He can help you find strength. He can help you press forward. He can help you when you are confused, sad, or lonely. He knows that your emotions drains your strength, leaving you numb and at times feeling hopeless. He knows how those tears well up out of nowhere and at unexpected times. He knows that every time that you think that you are in control, you lose control. He knows that there are times when the pain becomes so intense that you don't have words to explain it. He knows that you can not dismiss the pain, no matter how hard you try.

God is right there with outstretched arms. Fall into His arms, and there He will grant you a peace of mind, and a calming for your heart. Even Jesus cried out in deep anguish while on the cross to the Father, and Jesus expects us to cry out to Him. He is always available to us, listening to us, and is ready for us to cry out our sadness and heartbreaks.

THE DOMINO EFFECT

The Domino Effect is the cumulative effect produced when one event sets off a chain of similar events. This term is best known as a mechanical effect and is used as an analogy to a falling row of dominoes.

The Domino Effect can easily be visualized by placing a row of dominoes upright, each separated by a small space. When you push the first domino, the next domino in line will be knocked down, and so on.

Playing with dominoes is so exciting. Setting them up on a table or floor, and then seeing if they will fall in the order that you desire, is amazing. Dominoes teaches us about process, sequence, and the way things work. You learn from dominoes, that you have to have a starting point. You don't start in the middle. You have to have enough space between each domino to cause an effective chain of reaction. Dominoes teaches us about cause and effect and about the impact of a chain of events.

In essence, the domino effect begins with one domino, that has an impact on another, so that the original domino, not only impacts one other domino, but it impacts ALL of the other dominoes as well.

Case in point, the first Domino Effect ever, Adam and Eve. When God placed Adam and Eve in the garden, He gave them crystal clear instructions. He told Adam, "You may surely eat of every tree of the garden, but of the tree of the knowledge of good and evil you shall not eat, for in the day that you eat of it you shall surely die" (Genesis 2:16-17). So when the serpent approached Eve, he asked her, "Did God really say you must not eat from any tree in the garden?" Eve explained to him that God had commanded them that they may eat from any tree in the garden, but not from the tree in the center of the garden (the tree of the knowledge of good and evil). "God said that we must not eat it or even touch it, or we will die." The serpent responded, "You will not surely die...For God knows that when you eat of it your eyes will be opened and you will be like God, knowing good and evil" (Genesis 3:4-5).

The serpent got Eve to concentrate on the pleasures of the eye, "the woman saw that the fruit of the tree was good for food and pleasing to the eye." Then the serpent glamorized what would happen if she ate it, "For God knows that in the day you eat from it your eyes will be opened, and you will be like God, knowing good and evil." Eve took some fruit and ate it and then gave some to Adam and he ate it. Eating the forbidden fruit was a domino effect, because there were some dire consequences for them and some dire consequences that affected everything and everyone. Their disobedience affected all humanity and all creation.

When Adam disobeyed God, Adam brought sin and death to all people. The result of his sin separated them from God and eventually death, sickness, and destruction to all creation. But just as one man brought sin into the world, because of God's grace, He provided us with a gift of grace, through one Man, Jesus Christ. We have death through Adam and life through Christ: "But the gift is not like the trespass. For if the many died by the trespass of the one man, how much more did God's grace and the gift that came by the grace of the one man, Jesus Christ, overflow to the many! Again, the gift of God is not noke the result of the one man's sin: The judgment followed one sin and brought condemnation, but the gift followed many trespasses and brought justification. For if, by the trespass of the one man, death reigned through that one man, how much more will those who receive God's abundant provision of grace and of the gift of righteousness reign in life through the one man, Jesus Christ" (Romans 5:15-17).

Praise God for Jesus Christ, our Redeemer. When Adam and Eve set this chain reaction of dominoes into motion, Jesus said: "I am the resurrection and the life, he who believes in Me, though he may die, he shall live. And whoever lives and believes in Me shall never die." (John 11:25)

> "I am the good shepherd. The good shepherd lays down his life for the sheep." (John 10:11)

> "I am the way, the truth, and the life. No one comes to the Father except through Me." (John 14:6)

"I am the door. If anyone enters by Me, he will be saved, and will go in and find pasture...I have come that they may have life, and that they may have it more abundantly." (John 10:9)

"I am the living bread which came down from heaven. If anyone eats of this bread, he will live forever; and the bread that I shall give is My flesh, which I shall give for the life of the world." (John 6:51)

The Domino Effect is very real. One decision triggers other decisions and choices, which will result in going down a particular pathway based on your original decision. That's why you want the dominoes that fall in your life to be in line with what God wants best for you. God knows how one domino leads to another domino, and the choices we make could be a blessing or a curse. That is why being obedient and committed to Jesus is critical.

The Bible makes it crystal clear about explaining the cause and effects of choices we make in life. There are warnings throughout the entire Bible about the consequences of sin and its domino effect it will have on us. The Bible also explains how the domino effect of obedience can lead to blessings in this life and eternity.

Every decision or choice we make is very important, because each decision will almost have an inescapable consequence, because it may affect your destiny in life and eternity. Everything we do in life should start with God and the Word of God. If you desire to please and glorify God, make your decisions based on the Bible. Allow your life to reflect the image of Christ and obey

His commands. Remember, God is using you as an instrument to reach others for Him. What a Domino Effect!

"There is one body and one Spirit; just as also you were called in one hope of your calling; one Lord, one faith, one baptism, one God and Father of all who is above all, and through all, and in you all" (Ephesians 4:4-6).

GOOD MORNING, HEARTBREAK!

HEARTBREAK! Who hasn't had their heart broken? I remember my first heartbreak like it was yesterday. I was devastated, to say the least. I must have cried about it for over a year. In hindsight, God did me a tremendous favor when He forced him out of my life. Then God sent me the love of my life, my husband. We were married for over 43 blissful years, then my husband died of cancer. Oh what a heartbreak! Rev. Porter has been deceased now for several years and I am still wallowing in the Valley of Heartbreak.

Heartbreak! There is no set expiration date of recovery from a heartbreak. It is the worst feeling in the world, and ooh, so painful. It feels like your heart is literally breaking. Like your heart has been shattered into millions of tiny pieces. No one can describe the pain of how you feel. That pain is different for each individual.

All you want is them, the one you lost. You now realize that you can't be with them any more and you can't move on without them. You can't sleep because of the pain and tears. It feels like the world is coming to an end, at least your world. You don't know what to do with yourself, there are times that it may seem like there is no point in living, because nothing can make you happy.

Heartbreak! Are you experiencing a heartbreak? What is causing your heartbreak? Maybe it is the experience of a romantic break-up, infidelity, an end of a friendship, rejection, separation, someone could not reciprocate your love, illness, loss of job, change in lifestyle, loss of independence, or death. The pain of living without someone makes you feel shattered and broken.

A romantic heartbreak brings about a lot of pain because you gave your love, and being in love is the best euphoric emotion in the world. You will never enter into a relationship as a thought of getting your heart broken. No one knows what the future holds. But anytime you become emotionally involved with someone, you become a risk taker and that means there is a 50/50 chance that your heart will be broken.

Heartbreak! It seems as though my heartbreak is never ending. Every morning Heartbreak greets me with many gloomy disguises, and I simply say, "Good morning, Heartbreak." My bedroom feels like it is filled with a fragrance of disbelief. My pillow appears to be stuffed with an overwhelming feeling of broken-heartedness. My mattress appears to envelop me with never-ending lethargy. My pajamas feels like it has been washed in anguish, rinsed in misery, and dried in sadness. When I look in the mirror, Heartbreak stares at me with those sorrowful eyes. My face is being washed with a cleansing cream of emptiness. It's like I am brushing my teeth with toothpaste made of lack of interest. Even my clothes are throwing vibes of shock and unhappiness. While drinking my coffee, indifferent, trauma, disconnect, and distress, joins me to keep me company. And all throughout the day, loneliness, depression, sadness, and agony follows me everywhere I go. The only time that I can escape from Heartbreak is when I finally go to sleep. When morning comes, Heartbreak greets me again, and my reply is always the same, "Good morning, Heartbreak."

I know that time heals all things. I know that it will take time for my shattered broken heart to heal. My son Jay, constantly reminds me, "Mama you loved daddy so much and so very hard, your shattered broken heart is the price you paid for that kind of love." He is so correct. The harder you love, the more painful the loss.

"The LORD is close to the brokenhearted and saves those who are crushed in spirit" (Psalm 34:18).

MISERY LOVES COMPANY

Have you ever been miserable? Maybe you have never been miserable, but I am sure you have run across some people that were miserable. The word miserable is defined as a state or feeling of great distress or discomfort of mind or body.

Have you ever heard the phrase, "misery loves company?" Misery really loves company! A miserable person is a very unhappy person and they seek to make others miserable and unhappy too. Miserable people usually want other people around them to be as miserable as they are, so they can all have a massive misery/pity party. Some people find it extremely comforting when other people are going through the same things that they are going through. They seek the miserable company of others who are not satisfied, resentful, unhappy, and are complainers. These people are jealous hearted, hateful, bitter, feel dejected and defeated. They seek to be around like minded people.

Can you imagine the invitees at that massive misery/pity party? People have gathered there as a social past-time to share their misery with each other. It usually will offer some type of emotional release when they share their story. Imagine, while on the dance floor, each individual will display their dance of choice in some form of misery, such as agony, depression, suffering, torment, and the likes.

Imagine the banquet table full of entrees with platters full of despondency, bowls full of gloom, with sides of heartache. The table has a variety of dips filled with sorrow, worry, and melancholy. All of them are seasoned with a little bit of bad news. The salad bar consists of distress for lettuce, anxiety for tomatoes, woe for cucumbers, and affliction for croutons. The choice of salad dressings are wretchedness and unhappiness. The dessert table is filled with cakes made of torture, pies with discomfort, cookies with despair, and tarts full of grief. Each beverage represents a combination of sadness, anguish, hurt, and pain.

People this miserable are usually looking for targets to be the object of their attacks. They will criticize or belittle you. They will say some of the cruelest words to you. They will look at you and think that you did something wrong to them, but that miserable person is only looking for an outlet. Sometimes it may come from a complete stranger or someone you just met, but don't be surprise when it comes from your closet friend or a family member. Believe me, I have received attacks from each one of those scenarios. So when their tongues start lashing out those hateful and hurtful words, I then realize that it's my job as a Christian to pray for them.

Then I make a committed effort in knowing that Ms. or Mr. Misery, cannot request my company again. I thank God that I know Jesus.

Now let me be explicitly clear, everyone that is miserable is not trying to drag you down to hurt you or belittle you. They are just unhappy with their life, whether personal or professional. They are simply looking for a way out of their situation. They are searching for someone to help them. These people usually are not jealous hearted, vindictive, resentful, hateful or bitter, but most times they are just depressed or lonely and they need someone around them that they can relate to or vent to. God knows that at times we may suffer loneliness and depression. God knows that there will be times that we may be low in spirit. God is still there with us and He's not going anywhere, "The Lord is near to the brokenhearted and saves the crushed in spirit" (Psalm 34:18). This can be an excellent opportunity where you can reach out and help them that is reaching out for help.

I am a very positive person. I think positive things and I display an upbeat and positive posture. When I am feeling discouraged about anything, I always talk to the Lord about it. But everyone is not like me. Some people handle their problems and struggles in so many different ways. Problems and struggles are just a part of life, but take comfort in knowing that God is always there for us, no matter what troubles we may face. "Praise be to the God and Father of our Lord Jesus Christ, the Father of compassion and the God of all comfort, who comforts us in all troubles, so that we can comfort those in any trouble with the comfort we ourselves received from God" (2 Corinthians 1:3-4).

Yes, misery loves company and as long as YOU are not the company, then you have nothing to worry about.

THE LORD IS MY SHEPHERD

The Lord is my shepherd! Who is my shepherd? The **LORD** is my shepherd! The Lord is my Shepherd, and that excludes any other person or thing in this whole universe. The Lord **IS** my shepherd! The word **"IS"** speaks to a present relationship. The Lord is my Shepherd is implying that right now, I am under the Shepherd's care, who is Jesus Christ, my Lord and Savior. The Lord is **MY** Shepherd! The possessive word **"MY"** identifies as something which relates to those whose Shepherd truly is the Lord.

The Lord is MY Shepherd! Psalm 23 presents to us some mighty powerful promises from the Lord. Life is truly a journey with so many hills and valleys. Psalm 23 gives a tremendous promise of comfort, that on this life's journey, God will always be with us. God deeply cares about us and He will actively seek us, even if we get separated from the flock. Scripture reminds us,

"What man of you, having a hundred sheep, if he has lost one of them, does not leave the ninety-nine in the open country, and go after the one that is lost, until he finds it? And when he has found it, he lays it on his shoulders, rejoicing" (Luke 15:3-5).

The Lord is My Shepherd! He continually restores our wounded and troubled soul. He gives us strength and energizes us daily as we stay on the battlefield. He is greatly concern for those who are perishing, and Scripture reminds us, "He is patient with you, not wanting anyone to perish, but everyone to come to repentance." He desires to seek those who have been scattered because of the attacks from our enemy, Satan. We know from 2 Corinthians 1:20, "For no matter how many promises God has made, they are 'Yes' in Christ. And so through him the 'Amen' is spoken by us to the glory of God."

John 10 clearly reminds us that Jesus is the Good Shepherd. As the Good Shepherd, Jesus knows each and every sheep in His flock by name. He knows His sheep personally. His sheep knows His voice and listens when their name is called. They listen when He speaks. They listen for directions. They listen for instructions. They listen for comfort. They listen out of obedience. They listen because they know that He cares. They listen because He is the Good Shepherd. They listen because they know that Jesus loves them totally and completely unconditionally.

Jesus wants us to recognize Him both as our Shepherd and personally, as **MY** Shepherd. Jesus boldly says, "I am the Good Shepherd. The Good Shepherd lays down his life for the sheep" (John 10:11). Jesus said this twice in a very short sentence, that He laid down His life for all mankind. Jesus loves us so much that He wants us to know that His death was NOT a victory for His enemy. His death was a living sacrifice for us. He give up His life completely and voluntarily. It was done out of love. He finished His work on the cross and His resurrection was for our justification to salvation. Thankfully, whenever we sin, we have Jesus' blood to justify us. When we fall, we have His atoning sacrifice.

The Lord **IS** my Shepherd! Not was, or will be, or maybe, or fixin' to be, or going to be, or sometimes, or thinking about it. No! He **IS** my Shepherd right now, today, tomorrow, always and forevermore.

The Lord IS my Shepherd! Not maybe on Monday or Tuesday or Wednesday or only on some weekdays, or only on the weekends, or only on my birthday, or only on a holiday. No! He is my Shepherd everyday of the week, including birthdays and holidays.

The Lord IS my Shepherd! Not maybe in January, skip February, then again in March, then every other month after that. No! He is MY shepherd every month of the year, all year long.

The Lord IS my Shepherd! Not maybe just at home, or sometimes on the job, or at some select locations, or every other vacation, or maybe walking in the park, or sometimes in the car. No! He is my Shepherd everywhere I go and wherever I am.

The Lord IS my Shepherd! The Lord is my Shepherd, in illness, in health, during trouble times, in good times, in trials, in tribulations, in peace, in war, in disappointments, in silent times, in testing times, in uncertain times. He is my Shepherd at all times.

When the Lord is your Shepherd, you shall not want. John 6:35 says, "For I am the bread of life. He who comes to me will never go hungry, and he who believes in me will never be thirsty." Colossians 3:10 tells us, "And you have been given fullness in Christ, who is the head over every power and authority." Thus, you are complete in Him. When the Lord is your Shepherd, you shall never lack for anything, for we can be satisfied in Him, never lacking any good thing. It does not mean that you will have much material gain, but rather spiritually, you will lack nothing.

The Lord is my Shepherd! I do not lack. I cannot lack. I shall never lack, with Jesus as MY Shepherd. God will provide for me. God Himself is my Provision. God Himself is my Provider. God Himself is my Sustainer. All of my needs and all that I have, is because "The Lord is my Shepherd, I shall not want."

The Lord is my Shepherd! He is the One who tends and cares for all the basic needs of His sheep. He is the One who takes responsibility for the growth and welfare of His sheep. He is the One who protects, guides, and feeds His sheep.

The Lord IS my Shepherd! Who is your shepherd?

YOUR IMAGINATION

In the deep recess of our unconscious, there is a well of creativity. Creativity is the source of our imagination. In each of us there are hidden treasures and ideas just waiting to be tapped and discovered.

Imagination is the ability to form a mental image of something that is not perceived through the five senses; hearing, taste, smell, touch, and vision. It is the ability of the mind to build mental scenes, pictures, objects or events that do not exist, or not present, or have happened in the past. This ability can manifest in many forms and with our imagination, we can travel anywhere, and with no obstacles.

An imagination allows us the freedom to be as creative as we want to be. Our imagination allows us to be our truest self. You can visualize what you want to do, or be, build, or create, to your heart's desire.

We use our imagination even when we don't think that we are imagining anything. We daydream and fantasize all throughout the day. What a wonderful thing! Our imagination stirs our creative juices which allows us to create some unlimited ideas, dreams, and inspirations.

Our imagination is very powerful and God gave us this very powerful gift. An imagination is not bad or evil, but mankind is. We can use our imagination to become whatever we want to be. God gave us this wonderful gift, our imagination, and He meant for it to be used for good and not for evil. Your imagination can lead you to God or lead you away from God. Romans 1:21 says: "Because that, when they knew God, they glorified him not as God, neither were thankful, but became vain in their imaginations, and their foolish heart was darkened."

Beware of the tricks of the enemy, Satan. The enemy can manipulate your thoughts. He uses tricks and deceit and worldly mindsets to pervert believers in using their imagination in sinful and unhealthy ways. He will have you imagine false ideas about God. He will have you to imagine that money is your security blanket, instead of God. He will make you think that you are better than other people, through pride. He will have you to image all kinds of evil schemes to manipulate and take advantage of other people. He will have you image pessimistic, negative, fearful, and evil thoughts. Never forget who your enemy is and how he wish to destroy you. The Bible tells us, "For our struggle is not against flesh and blood, but against the rulers, against the authorities, against the powers of this dark world and against the spiritual forces of evil in the heavenly realms" (Ephesians 6:12). The problem arrives when you use your imagination to focus on sinful things. God did not give you your imagination to focus on evil thoughts. He wouldn't! He couldn't! He didn't! He never did nor never will!

God gave us the gift of imagination for a reason. For godly purposes. When you focus on God, in all things, you will find yourself using your imagination for God's glory. Your imagination can be used to show you how to help other people. Your imagination can be used in knowing how someone may feel when they are grieving, during an illness, suffering from disappointments, and dealing with life's challenges. Your imagination can show you how to support and encourage other people. Your imagination can be used in furthering God's kingdom. Your imagination is what you can use to captivate every thought toward the obedience of Christ Jesus. Your imagination can catapult you to be more Christ-like.

You know what? Faith uses our imagination. Faith allows us to see things that are not as though they were: "Now faith is the substance of things hoped for, the evidence of things not seen" (Hebrews 11:1). Faith confirms what we can only see through our imagination, because it has not come to fruition. God wants us to use our imagination in connection with our faith: "But without faith it is impossible to please him: for he that cometh to God must believe that he is, and that he is a rewarder of them that diligently seek him" (Hebrews 11:6).

Imagination allows you to turn your dreams into reality. There are no boundaries to your passion when you are under the influence of your imagination. You have wings when you live through imagination. Imagination rules the world. Imagination will take you to worlds that never were. If only you can imagine! "I can do all things through Christ which strengthen me" (Philippians 4:13). Can you imagine what you could or would do if only you can do all things through Christ? Imagine that!

RELATIONSHIPS

What is a relationship? A relationship is any connection between two people, which can be positive or negative. To be in a relationship doesn't always mean that there is physical intimacy, commitment, or emotional attachment. There are some very unique and different types of relationships, but the basic types of relationships will usually fall into categories. You have the family relationship, friendships, work related, platonic, situational (situationships), romantic, toxic, casual, codependent, open, sexual, long distance, and acquaintances.

We as human beings are naturally sociable. We all are in some form or in some type of relationship, be it family or otherwise. A good relationship will require trust, respect, communication, and self-awareness.

Trust: When you trust someone, you can be open and honest with them about your thoughts and actions. You shouldn't have to be worried about them being a "back-stabber."

Respect: When there is mutual respect, you will value each other's opinions.

Self-awareness: When there is self-awareness, you will take responsibility for your words and actions. You do not allow your negative emotions to impact the people around you.

Communications: This is extremely important. All good relationships depend on honest and open communications.

What type of relationship do you have with yourself? Your relationship that you have with yourself is very important. We are self-conscious human beings. We think about ourselves. We talk to ourselves. We judge ourselves. We are in a relationship with ourselves, whether we are happy or unhappy with ourselves. Self-esteem is what we think about ourselves.

When we have a positive self-esteem, we are confident and have self-respect. We are content with ourselves and our abilities to get things done, because we feel that we are competent. A healthy self-esteem makes our lives feel happy and joyful. It affects events in our life, including our relationships, goals, work, family, ourselves, and God.

When our self-esteem is negative, it affects all of our relationships, including ourselves. We will feel insecure. We will compare ourselves to others. We will doubt and criticize ourselves. We will not even recognize our self-worth nor will we express our own needs and wants. We can't handle or manage our life's disappointments.

What type of relationship do you have with God? Just like you value your relationship with your family, friends, spouse, or significant other, nothing or no one can replace your relationship with God. We were created to have a relationship with God. God requires an intimate relationship with us. He is our heavenly Father and He has plans for our life. "For I know the plans I have for you, says the Lord. They are plans for good and not for evil, to give you a future and a hope. In those days when you pray, I will listen. You will find me when you seek me, if you look for me in earnest" (Jeremiah 29:11-13).

God is our loving and merciful Father. He created you and me for His purpose. God is love and Jesus came to show us His love. God is our friend and we can go boldly before Him at anytime for any reason. God is sovereign, patient, and kind in dealing with us. God is omnipotent. He is all powerful. God never changes. He is holy. He answers our prayers, according to His will for us. God longs to visit with us. We were created to fellowship with Him. God protects us. God promotes us. God honors us. God lifts us up. We are precious in His sight because He loves us.

Like in any relationship, God wants us to read His love letter to us, the Bible. The Bible teaches us how to have a right and intimate relationship with God. He wants us to talk to Him by praying to Him. When we pray to Him, we are sharing what is on our heart. This is the time when we are spending time with Him, thanking Him and recognizing all He does for us. Then God wants us to listen to Him. He wants to share some intimate things with us that will help us in our life. He wants to provide us guidance for our life and help us to avoid the pitfalls of life. He wants to tell us how much He loves us. He wants us to know that we can trust Him. Scripture reminds us, "If you want favor with both God and man, and a reputation for good judgment and common sense, then trust the Lord completely; don't ever trust yourself. In everything you do, put God first, and he will direct you and crown your efforts with success" (Proverbs 3:5-6). When you do this, your relationship with God will be amazing and incredible. A life that only God can fulfill and give you. A life of joy and peace.

A DAMASCUS ROAD EXPERIENCE

"But Paul, threatening with every breath and eager to destroy every Christian, went to the High Priest in Jerusalem. He requested a letter addressed to synagogues in Damascus, requiring their cooperation in the persecution of any believers he found there, both men and women, so that he could bring them in chains to Jerusalem. As he was nearing Damascus on this mission, suddenly a brilliant light from heaven spotted down upon him! He fell to the ground and heard a voice saying to him, 'Paul! Paul! Why are you persecuting me?'" (Acts 9:1-6).

Paul was very religious. His training was the finest available. His intentions and efforts were not just sincere, but extremely sincere. He was a good Pharisee. He knew the scribes. He sincerely believed that this new movement, Christianity was dangerous to Judaism. Thusly, Paul hated Christians and their new Christian faith called the Way. So without mercy, he persecuted Christians. He was even at the persecution of Stephen. He got permission to travel to Damascus to capture Christians and to bring them back to Jerusalem. But God stopped him dead in his tracks. On the Damascus Road Paul personally met Jesus Christ and his life was never the same.

"For all have sinned, and come short of the glory of God" (Romans 3:23). Since the beginning of mankind, every human that has been born was born with a sinful nature. Why do you think Jesus Christ had to leave His regal throne in heaven to come to earth, died in our place, and rose again to conquer death and sin? Jesus provides us the gift of salvation, as a gift to all who will take it. When we come to Jesus, confess our sins, repent thereof, by turning away from them, and when we seek His ways, we experience a total transformation. This encounter with Jesus transforms us.

What is a Damascus Road Experience? It is an epiphany or a certain turning point in your life. It comes from the Apostle Paul's experience on Damascus Road. Figuratively, a Damascus Experience means to have a life changing encounter with God. You take a 180 degree turn from a path of sinning to an entirely new path for Christ. When you encounter Jesus on Damascus Road, you wholeheartedly will turn to Him in genuine repentance and faith. It's turning your back from the world and the worldly to follow after Christ and what is pleasing to him. You will desire to be in the will of the Lord. You will desire to become more like Him. You will desire to be obedient to Him. You will have a thirst for Christ and the willingness to have an intimate relationship with Him. You will desire to serve and help others, as you display your Christ likeness to others.

After Paul's conversion, he became a mighty ambassador for Christ. He worked hard to convince the Jews that Gentiles were acceptable to God, but he spent even more time convincing Gentiles that they were acceptable to God. The lives Paul touched were changed and challenged by meeting Christ through him. God did not waste any part of Paul. He used his background, his training, his citizenship, his mind, and his weaknesses to minister to all.

If you have ever had a Damascus Road experience, it was not just a 180 degree turnaround experience. It was a spiritual turning away from sin and to Christ by faith. It was a dramatic turning away from one path in order to purse an entirely new one. An entirely different one.

It involved a complete about-face, in order to enter through the narrow gate that leads to life. Matthew 7:13 says, "You can enter God's Kingdom only through the narrow gate. The highways to hell is broad, and its gate is wide for the many who choose that way."

It is not a partial change where you are able to straddle the fence. It is not a superficial change with a mere outward facade of your personal life to impress others. It is to break away from the old you from sinning, then embrace the new you, in Jesus Christ. This change is so profound that it involves a change of mind, a change of view, a new recognition of God and yourself. It involves an emotional change, a feeling of sorrow for your sins that were committed against a holy and righteous God. It is an intentional turning away from sin and a turning toward God through Jesus Christ. This involves the entire person, that means, all of you. You have turned your entire mind, your will, your affections, and your love, toward God. It's having an intimate and a right relationship with God.

The Damascus Road experience whole purpose is to bring men and women into a intimate and right relationship with God. This is why Jesus died for us. It was God who was "in Christ, reconciling the world unto Himself" (2 Corinthians 5:19).

LOVE!

What is love? Love is defined as a strong affection for another; a profoundly tender, passionate affection for another person; a feeling of warm personal attachment or deep affection as a parent, child, or friend. Love is often categorized in terms of types of relationship, such as romantic love, platonic love, etc. Love is often described as how serious or deep it is, like true love, unconditional love or if its reciprocated, as in unrequited love.

Synonyms for love implies different levels of intensity or intimacy such as affection, devotion, friendship, infatuation, lust, passion, tenderness, fondness and adoration.

We were created to love and to love each other. People think that love is a matter of the heart, but the main organ that is affected by love is actually the brain. The hormones our brain releases when we experience love leads to euphoria. It makes you feel like you have butterflies in your stomach. You know, that giddy feeling you feel when that person you like is around you.

There are different types of love and each love affects us differently and uniquely. Storge, Pragma, Philia, Eros, Philautia, Compassionate, Platonic, Obsessive, Ludus, Conjugal, and Agape have been classified as the different types of love.

Storge or Familiar Love, is love that flows between parents and children or childhood friends.

Pragma or Enduring Love, is love that matures over many years. It is a type of love where a couple chooses to put effort in their relationships. Instead of "falling in love," they are "standing in love."

Philia or Affectionate Love, is love without a romantic attraction. It occurs between friends or family members.

Eros or Romantic Love, is love that comes as a natural instinct. It is a passionate love that is displayed through physical affection, such as kissing, hugging, and holding hands.

Philautia or Self-Love, is having a healthy form of love towards yourself, where you love, respect, accept and appreciate yourself.

Compassionate Love, is love filled with emotional intimacy.

Platonic Love, is the simplest of all types of love. There are no sexual or romantic intentions.

Mania or Obsessive Love, is an obsessive love towards a partner. It leads to jealousy or possessiveness.

Ludus or Playful Love, is a child-like and flirtatious love that is normally found in the beginning stages of a relationship. It consists of teasing, playfulness and laughter between couples.

Conjugal Love, is also called companionate love. It is intimacy and commitment without passion.

Agape or Selfless Love, is the highest level of love to offer. It is a love that is not concerned about self and is concerned with the greatest good of another. It is not born out of emotions, feelings, familiarity, or attraction, but from the will and as a choice. Agape requires faithfulness, commitment, and sacrifice without expecting anything in return.

In the Bible, Agape love is the love that comes from God. "Beloved, let us love one another, for love is from God; and everyone who loves is born of God and knows God. The one who does not love does not know God, for God is love. By this the love of God was manifested in us, that God has sent His only begotten Son into the world so that we might live through Him. In this is love, not that we loved God, but that He loved us and sent His Son to be the propitiation for our sins. Beloved, if God so loved us, we also ought to love one another. No one has seen God at any time; if we love one another, God abides in us, and His love is perfected in us" (1 John 4:7-11).

Agape love is loving unconditionally. It is the highest form of love, "charity" and "the love, of God for man and of man for God." It comes out of a pure heart, a good conscience, and genuine faith. Agape love perfectly describes the kind of love Jesus Christ has for His Father and for us. Jesus displayed His love for us by sacrificing Himself on the cross for the sins of the world. Agape love defines God's perfect, unconditional, immeasurable, incomparable love for us. Agape love is God's outgoing, ongoing, selfless, and self-sacrificing love and concerns for you and me. NOW THAT'S LOVE!

WHAT KIND OF EXAMPLE ARE YOU?

As a Christian we must ask ourselves this question, "What kind of example am I?" Are you a Christian example in your speech? Are you a Christian example in your conduct? Are you a Christian example in showing love? Are you a Christian example in faith? Are you a Christian example whose life serves as a positive role model and whose actions are based on purity, fidelity, integrity, and the love for the Lord?

Are you a Christian example in speech? In speech, our words reflects our thoughts which reflects our hearts. Words can destroy someone and words can build someone up. "The good man brings good things out of the good stored up in him, and the evil man brings evil things out of the evil stored up in him. But I tell you that men will have to give account on the day of judgment for every careless word they have spoken. For by your words you will be condemned" (Matthew 12:35-37).

Words have energy and power with the ability to harm, to help, to hurt, to humble, or to humiliate. Have you ever had a conversation with someone and still today can remember that conversation, verbatim? Now, consider your conversations with someone, your words could change their whole life for the better or for the worse. The words we choose to use have meaning, whether negative or positive. If words have meaning, then believe me they will be remembered. WORDS. They are powerful. So choose your words wisely. Be mindful of the words you use.

Are you a Christian example in conduct? As Christians, we are called to be set apart from the world, so that when people see us, they will know that we represent Jesus. Our conduct in the Bible is called, "walk." Then how should we "walk?" Morally and spiritually. Philippians 1:27a tells us, "Whatever happens, conduct yourselves in a manner worthy of the gospel of Christ..." This includes our conduct in all areas of our life. I know that there are a lot of professed Christians that act worldly. We can't take responsibility for them, we can only take responsibility for ourselves. The Bible delineate our Christian Code of Conduct. Matter-of-fact, Romans 12 is titled, "A Living Sacrifice to God." It explains to us in explicit details how God is expecting us to live. This applies to our conduct, to any transaction, to how we dress, even to our style of living. There is nothing we can say or do that can be exempted from Romans 12. We are ambassadors of Jesus Christ and we need to act as so.

Are you a Christian example in love? How can you say the right words and live the right way, but do not love? "He who does not love does not know God, for God is love" (1 John 4:8). WE are commanded to love everyone including our enemies. What, my enemies too? Yes, and even those we find unlikeable. Our problem is that we misunderstand the word LOVE. The kind of love that we need in order to love people we don't even like is, AGAPE love. God's kind of love. Agape love is not a feeling. Although we can experience some mighty good feelings as a result of Agape love. Agape love does not depend on how we feel nor how others feel about us. Agape love is an action. Agape love says, "I love you in spite of..." In spite of things about you that I don't like. We are commanded to love others.

Are you a Christian example in faith? "Now faith is being sure of what we hope for and certain of what we do not see..." (Hebrews 11:1a). In this verse, we understand that faith is a confidence in things that are not visible and yet they are as real to us as the things that we can see. When we put our faith in God, we acknowledge Him as Sovereign over all things. After all He is the Creator and Sustainer of life. He wants us to completely trust Him by resting in Him, by placing our faith in Him and Him only, not in anyone, not in ourselves, nor our abilities, but in Him and His abilities. Remember, without faith it is impossible to please God, because anyone who comes to Him must believe that He exists and He is the Rewarder of those who earnestly seek Him. When we place our faith in God, we demonstrate that we believe His Word and that we trust Him.

As a Christian, a follower of Christ, we must show Christ to the world by being a Christ-like example. A nonbeliever should be able to see Christ in us and should be so drawn to our light that they would desire to seek Christ and His salvation.

What kind of example are you?

WHEN EVIL HAS A FACE

Evilness is all around us. Evilness is the quality of being morally wrong in practice or principle. In this world people are displaying so much hate, anger, and being mean-spirited. It's like, anything goes. When one think of evilness you begin to think of images from mythology, books, and movies that portrays evil as personified in spiritual forces. Maybe a demon possess haunted house, exorcism by sprinkling of holy water, or spirits summoned by an Quija board.

Evil is real and present in this sin filled world and it seems like evilness has been "TURNED-UP." Just look around you. Turn on the TV and listen to the news. So what is going on? It's what has been going on since the beginning of time. We first read about evil in the Bible in Genesis 2:17, "But the tree of the Knowledge of good and evil, thou shalt not eat of it; for in the day that thou eat thereof thou shall surely die."

When God created mankind He gave us free-will with the ability to choose between good and evil. When Adam and Eve sinned, sin entered into the world, as well as judgment. This judgment was extended not just to man, but to Satan as well. Satan deceived mankind then, and he continues to do so now. When you look at the world, from social media to politics, you would be blind not to see the power of the devil. Satan is at work everywhere.

Evilness is anything that contradicts the Holy nature of God, because God is Holy. Those who practice evil are in Satan's family. God hates wicked people and Psalm 11:5 makes it plain, "The LORD test the righteous, but his soul hates wicked and the one who loves violence." God hates their ways, their thoughts, their actions, and their evil deeds.

Anytime you are confronted by betrayal, hatred, rage, lies, cruelty, deceitfulness, evilness of any kind, and you realized who did it to you, be it family, friend, or foe, now you can place a face on who did the evil deed. Evil now has a face.

THE WAITING SEASON

WAITING! Are you in a "waiting season?" If you are not, then you are truly blessed.

The "waiting season" skips no one, it hasn't knock on your door yet. Sometimes pain is in your season of waiting. I am currently in my "waiting season," and pain is in my season of waiting. Yet, I realize and recognize that whatever I am waiting for is out of my control. I am going through a lot of tribulation. I can't run from it and I can't hide from it. It is something that I must go through.

In the midst of this chaos, I must stop and give God the glory, because I have peace in my "waiting season." Maybe I have accepted where I am and find myself being present here. Waiting seasons have its struggles, but there are blessings in it as well.

"The Lord is my shepherd; I shall not want. He <u>makes</u> me lie down in green pastures. He <u>leads</u> me beside the <u>still</u> waters. He

<u>restores</u> my soul" (Psalm 23:1-2). Psalm 23 is about the LORD comforting and reassuring us about His provision for us. I have realized that I am not where I am by accident. I have learned that in my waiting, it has pushed me into having a deeper and more intimate relationship with Jesus. Pulling from Psalm 23, in my "waiting season," He has <u>made</u> me lie down in green pastures, while He <u>leads</u> me beside the <u>still</u> waters. In this stillness, I am being <u>restored</u> from the difficulties of grief, betrayal, and wrong doings.

In the <u>stillness</u>, God has given me peace and in Him I have found <u>rest</u>. I wait in <u>stillness</u>. In this <u>stillness</u>, God is here. He is not requiring any work from me, because He doesn't need any help from me. He just want me to <u>rest</u> in Him. He wants me to trust Him. He wants me to patiently wait on Him. He wants me to be <u>STILL</u>. The LORD is at work! Although I can't see anything happening in my life right now, but I know that He is working it out for my good. "The Lord is good to those who wait for him, to the soul who seeks Him" (Lamentations 3:25).

If you are in a "waiting season," this waiting season of your life is producing something in you. When you get where God needs for you to be, I wonder what parts of you God have refined, and how it made you better able to create, teach, learn, follow, lead, comfort, and love, because of this season.

God is digging a well for you. God is cultivating a well that you will draw from for the rest of your life. He is digging that well to fill it with hope, grace, kindness, patience, love, and wisdom. Sometimes this can only happen during a very painful season of waiting.

I wonder what you will be like when the waiting is over. I wonder what part of you HE would have refined. Please don't try to rush God's timetable and His process. If you want a meaningful and fruitful life, it cannot be found in the grandiose moments of life. It is only found in the sacrificial preparations of life. Deep in the valley of life.

This season of waiting is producing things in you that will help you be a better you. A more trusting in the Lord, you. You will be a better you because you have learned how to suffer well.

Keep waiting on the Lord Jesus. He is walking with you. He is talking to you. He is holding you and He is never letting go. Trust me, Jesus is working it out for your good in this waiting season.

SUFFERING!

Are you suffering? Everyone suffers somehow, in some form, in some fashion, at some time. Suffering is an inevitable part of life, from aging, death, heartbreak, and through disappointments. We suffer from physical pain, injury, and disease. We have emotional suffering through betrayal, loneliness, rejection, and all the traumas of life. And yet, suffering seems to be one of the great instruments of God. How? Suffering continues to reveal to us our dependence on God. Not only our dependence on Him, but our hope in Him, despite of our circumstances. Suffering deepens our faith and our spiritual experience.

How can you comfort someone else unless God put you in training? And how does God train you? He allows you to suffer. Oh, I truly know that training is costly, and sometimes extreme. In order to be perfect in ministry, you must go through the same afflictions that many other believers have gone through or will go through. God comforts the suffering through fellow-sufferers. Paul says that this is one of God's plans for our pain: "What a wonderful God we have - he is the Father of our Lord Jesus Christ, the source of every mercy, and the one who so wonderfully comforts and strengthens us in our hardships and trails. And why does he do this? So that when others are troubled, needing our sympathy and encouragement, we can pass on to them this same help and comfort God has given us. You can be sure that the more we undergo sufferings for Christ, the more he will shower us with his comfort and encouragement" (2 Corinthians 1:3-5).

Through suffering your life becomes the hospital where God will teach you the divine art of comfort. Take the story of Joseph, for example. Joseph experienced his share of suffering in his early years. He suffered the spitefulness of jealousy from his brothers. He was sold to slave traders, then falsely accused of rape by Potiphar's wife, and wrongfully jailed for a crime that he didn't commit.

Through all of this, God wasn't absent from him. God was ever present in his life. He suffered being in prison, but God place him in charge of the whole land of Egypt. The evidence of the Spirit of God was in his life. God's Spirit bore the fruit of righteousness through Joseph in Egypt. Could such fruit have been produced without the suffering? Probably not. "When your faith is tested, your endurance has a chance to grow. So let it grow, for when your endurance is fully developed, you will be strong in character and ready for anything" (James 1:3-4).

So do you wonder why you are facing a special sorrow? When this special sorrow has passed, you will find many others that are experiencing your type of special sorrow. You will tell them how you suffered and how you were comforted. Then as your story unfolds, you will tell them how God wrapped His arms around you. You will tell them how He gave you a gleam of hope and how He chased the shadows of despair from you. "In all this you greatly rejoice, though now for a little while you may have had to suffer grief in all kinds of trials. These have come so that the proven genuineness of faith - of greater worth than gold, which perishes even though refined by fire - may result in praise, glory and honor when Jesus Christ is revealed" (1 Peter 1:6-7).

God comforts us so that we can comfort others.

God grants us mercy so that we can be merciful to others.

God helps us in our suffering so that we can help others in theirs.

God would never leave us alone in our suffering, so we shouldn't leave others alone in theirs.

When we are affected and have to suffer, God is allowing us to have the experience so that we can be helpful to others. Our suffering is a character builder. In suffering, God can make us fruitful. When we are fruitful, we can be ready for anything.

God didn't promise us that He would make us comfortable in this life, but He does want us to comfort the comfortless.

GOD KEEPS HIS PROMISES!

Look at any word or promise in the Bible that God has spoken, then underscore it with ME, MINE, and MY. That word is a promise to you. Now put your finger on any of God's promises and say, "IT'S MINE!" Our heavenly father has already endorsed it. You must believe that, "IT IS DONE." Guess what? Jesus has "FULFILLED IT IN YOU!"

God promised us that He is kind and compassionate - "Though the mountains be shaken and the hills be removed, yet my unfailing love (kindness) for you will not be shaken nor my covenant of peace be removed, says the Lord, who has compassion on you" (Isaiah 54:10).

God promised us that He would help us - "So do not fear, for I am with you; do not be dismayed, for I am your God. I will strengthen you and help you; I will uphold you with my righteous right hand" (Isaiah 41:10).

God promised to strengthen us - "For this reason I bow my knees before the Father, from whom every family in heaven and on earth is named, that according to the riches of his glory he may grant you to be strengthened with power through his Spirit in your inner being" (Ephesians 3:14-16).

God promised that He would guide us - "This is what the Lord says - your Redeemer, the Holy One of Israel: 'I am the Lord your God, who teaches you what is best for you, who directs you in the way you should go'" (Isaiah 48:17).

God promised us salvation - "If you confess with your mouth, 'Jesus is Lord,' and believe in your heart that God raised Him from the dead, you will be saved. One believes with the heart, resulting in righteousness, and one confesses with the mouth, resulting in salvation" (Romans 10:9-10).

God promised us that He has plans for us - "For I know the plans I have for you," declares the LORD, "Plans to prosper you and not to harm you, plans to give you hope and a future" (Jeremiah 29:11).

God promised us that He would meet our needs - "And my God will meet all your needs according to the riches of his glory in Christ Jesus" (Philippians 4:19).

God promised us that He is our refuge - "The LORD is a refuge for the oppressed, a stronghold in times of trouble. Those who know your name trust in you, for you, LORD, have never forsaken those who seek you" (Psalm 9:9-10).

God promised to be with us - "Have I not commanded you? Be strong and courageous. Do not be frightened, and do not be dismayed, for the Lord your God is with you wherever you go" (Joshua 1:9).

God promised to give us rest - "Then Jesus said, 'Come to me, all of you who are weary and carry heavy burdens, and I will give you rest. Take my yoke upon you. Let me teach you, because I am humble and gentle at heart, and you will find rest for your souls. For my yoke is easy to bear, and the burden I give you is light" (Matthew 11:28-30).

God promised us that He would be with us in times of trouble - "He shall call upon Me, and I will answer him; I will be with him in trouble; I will deliver him and honor him. With long life I will satisfy him, and show him My salvation" (Psalm 91:15-16)

God promised us His Provision - "This is why I tell you: Don't worry about your life, what you will eat or what you will drink; or about your body, what you will wear. Isn't life more than food and the body more than clothing? Look at the birds of the sky: They don't sow or reap or gather into barns, yet your heavenly Father feeds them. Aren't you worth more than they?" (Matthew 6:25-26)

God promised us that we can ask Him for anything - "So I say to you: Ask and it will be given to you; seek and you will find; knock and the door will be opened to you. For everyone who asks receives; the one who seeks finds; and to the one who knocks, the door will be opened" (Luke 11:9-10).

God promised to answers our prayers - "Whatever you ask in my name, I will do it so that the Father may be glorified in the Son. If you ask me anything in my name, I will do it" (John 14:13-14).

God promised to work everything out for our good - "And we know that all that happens to us is working for our good if we love God and are fitting into his plans" (Romans 8:28).

God promised us an abundant life - "The thief comes only to steal and kill and destroy; I came that they may have life, and have it abundantly" (John 10:10).

God promised love for us - "But God, being rich in mercy, because of His great love with which He loved us, even when we were dead in our transgressions, made us alive together with Christ (by grace you have been saved)" (Ephesians 2:4-5).

God promised that nothing can separate us from Him - "For I am sure that neither death nor life, nor angels nor rulers, nor things present nor things to come, nor powers, nor height nor depth, nor anything else in all creation, will be able to separate us from the love of God in Christ Jesus our Lord" (Romans 8:38-39).

God promised us everlasting life - "For God so loved the world, that he gave his only Son, that whoever believes in him should not perish but have eternal life" (John 3:16).

The Bible is full of promises that God has made to us. God has promised us some many things: His help and guidance, His faithfulness, Our salvation, Wisdom, Peace, Joy, Love, Riches in heaven, Adoption into his family, Strength, Power, His provision, Eternal life, Deliverance from enemies, Deliverance from danger, Deliverance from temptation, Healing and Renewal.

When we know what promises God has promised us, we can confidently claim His promises to us in our own lives. God can be trusted to deliver all of His promises, "Let us hold tightly without wavering to the hope we affirm, for God can be trusted to keep his promise" (Hebrews 10:23)

Amen and Praise the Lord!

THE TAPESTRY OF BITTERNESS

Bitterness is defined as anger and disappointment at being treated unfairly. It is an attitude of intense and prolonged anger and hostility which is synonymous with resentment and envy.

Bitterness is a spiritual sickness. It will consume you and is extremely dangerous to your emotional health. The Bible teaches us to, "Let all bitterness and wrath and anger and clamor and slander be put away from you, along with all malice" (Ephesians 4:31). Bitterness has the power to destroy us from within and can impact those around us negatively. Bitterness can harm us physically, emotionally, and spiritually. It will not allow us to feel God's peace. The more we hold onto those hurts, the more we become intoxicated on the pain. It affects you physically, emotionally, and spiritually, because it is an evil fruit that will truly destroy you.

Bitterness takes root in a heart that refuses to forgive and allows it to wallow in self-pity. Bitterness is a root that is hidden under the surface, then suddenly grows until it shows its ugly head. This is the nature of bitterness. It grows quietly in a wounded heart and is usually undetected. It occurs when we feel that someone has taken something from us, that we are powerless to get back. We hold on to hurt and pain in an attempt to remind ourselves and others of the injustice we have experienced. Bitterness only makes our sense of injustice, grow. It does not heal the wound caused by the injustice. It causes the wound to become infected with anger and hate.

Bitterness starts out small. We start replaying that situation over and over again in our minds, creating deeper and deeper wounds. We will retell our painful situation to anyone that is available to listen, and will include every bit of sordid detail. This pushes the resentment into a deeper and more painful embedded wound. Even when we hear the person's name that wounded us, we cringe and the wound starts spreading even more. We look for any reason, whether real or imagined to dislike the person even more. Every time we hit the mental replay button, we form another layer of bitterness. Bitterness is like a colony of termites that will eat at you from within.

Some people think that they have the right to be bitter. Bitterness is a choice! God can help you with everything that you go through, and it all starts with forgiveness. Forgiveness is a commitment. Forgiveness is releasing your rights to what you think that you are due. Forgiveness is releasing your rights to any kind of retaliation. Forgiveness is releasing your rights to keep bringing it up. Forgiveness is releasing your rights to stop hitting that mental replay button. Just like bitterness is a choice, forgiveness is a choice.

Bitterness makes you walk in the flesh and not in the Spirit. You have the choice every day to whether you will walk in the flesh or in the Spirit. You know whether or not you are walking in the flesh or the Spirit, when you start thinking about someone and don't feel joy and peace. You know when you are walking in the Spirit when they are no longer on your hit list. Don't give anybody that kind of power over you. I have read that 90% of all people in an insane asylum could be released if they would just learn how to forgive or be forgiven. We can't control what happens in our life, but we can control how we respond and react to what happens to us.

Forgiveness does not mean that everything is okay nor does it means pretending that everything is okay. It is a gift that you give yourself, that will enable you to stop picking at that wound and allow God to heal you. Only God can help you heal. He can help you choose not to remember the hurt and pain. It is a choice that only you can make. But why remain bitter? It is costly to remain bitter, but it is more costly not to forgive. Forgiveness is hard, but it will set you free. "For if you forgive men their trespasses, your heavenly Father will also forgive you. But if you do not forgive men their trespasses, neither will your Father forgive your trespasses" (Matthew 6:14-15).

Forgive or not to forgive, only you can make that choice. It's your choice to make.

SURRENDING ALL

What does "surrender" means? Surrender means to relinquish possession or control over. It is an act of surrendering, submission into the possession of another; abandonment, resignation. But what does "surrender" means spiritually? It means simply to let go and let God. In others words, to let go of control and to completely trust God in every situation. It means yielding control to what we consider ours; our lives, our possessions, our time, our problems, and our rights.

To be completely honest with you, you don't control anything anyway, because God controls everything. The truth is, He is always in control. It's just that the thought has not taken place in your mind yet. When you have not submitted to Him, then you have not surrendered to Him. Surrender implies loss or defeat to those who surrender, but we are called to surrender. This is the essence of beginning the Christian life.

It's not about "what you want to do" but, "what does God want you to do." In surrendering, we give up the notion that we know what is best for us, thereby LETTING GO and trusting what God knows what is best for us. It's not what we want to do with our lives, but what does God want for you and what does He want to do with your life, your possessions, and with your future.

When you pray the Lord's Prayer, "Thy kingdom come. Thy will be done in earth, as it is in heaven" (Matthew 6:10), this includes you, me, our life, our family, and our future. This is doing the will of God. It is only when we surrender, that God can do for us and with us, what He wants to do. When you commit to something, you are in control and you are trying to put in the efforts to make it successful. But when you surrender it to God, you have given the control to God, the ONE who can truly make it successful. Blessings come when you give up control to God. What a relief it is when you are not in control with your problems, your circumstances, your health, your life, and your trials. This is when you will find joy and peace. Even in the midst of your trials and tests.

You can only experience a truly fulfilled life when you surrender your life to God. Without surrendering, you will never live your life to its full potential. You are at your worst when you don't surrender everything to God, because you are not living God's will for your life. "Then he said to them all: 'If anyone would come after me, he must deny himself and take up his cross daily and follow me. For whoever wants to save his life will lose it, but whoever loses his life for me will save it'" (Luke 9:23-24).

"Letting go and letting God" take over our lives, is an everyday surrendering to Him, and sometimes having to do it many times throughout the day. We are always confronted with problems and needs, and we should seek God and give them all to Him. We are not to hold on to some of them and give Him some, but to give them all to Him. This is not about how committed you are, but how "surrendering" you need to be. Your daily practice and prayer should be, "Lord, I am going to give it all to you, by faith." The Bible truly tells us, "Now to Him who is able to do exceedingly abundantly above all that we ask or think, according to the power that works in us" (Ephesians 3:20). This is crystal clear, God is able to do EXCEEDINGLY ABUNDANTLY above all that we could ever ask or think, is an inexhaustible fullness of grace and mercy in God's love toward us. Whatever we may ask, or think, God is able to do it more abundantly, and exceedingly abundantly. So "letting go and letting God" should be our daily mantra. So, surrender it all to Jesus!

All to Jesus I surrender
All to Him I freely give
I will ever love and trust Him
In His presence daily live

All to Jesus I surrender
Humbly at His feet I bow
Worldly pleasures all forsaken
Take me, Jesus, take me now

I surrender all
I surrender all
All to Thee my blessed Savior
I surrender all

                        (Lyricist Judson W. Van DeVenter)

BROKENNESS

God uses us the most when we are broken. If the truth be told, all of us are broken in some way or another. We look at someone's outward appearance and they appear to have it going on and are all put together, but we can't see what's really happening on the inside.

We all have been broken. We have been broken by others and by people of this sin sick world. God loves to use broken people by restoring them and uses them for His glory.

The Bible is full of stories about brokenness. Take the story of Jacob. When Jacob was left alone, a Man wrestled with him until dawn. When the Man saw that He couldn't overpower him, He struck Jacob's hip, and knocked it out of joint. Jacob had fought with his brother Esau and won. He had fought with his uncle Laban and won. Now he fought against a "Man" that he could not defeat, and the "Man" crippled him in the fight. This "Man" was a Supernatural Being. Jacob tried to live his life his own way. He tried to run from God. He had an encounter with God and realizing he is wrestling with God, he requests a blessing. This is when God changed Jacob's name to Israel - meaning "strives for God." It was the brokenness of Jacob's natural strength that got Jacob where God could give him spiritual power. You see, there is no blessing without brokenness.

If you want a blessing, you must allow God to break you, thus brokenness. This has been true of all of God's servants in the Bible. Before God could use Moses to deliver His people out of Egypt, God had to put him in the desert for 40 years, taking care of sheep.

When Naomi lost her husband and two sons, she went through a period or brokenness. She even changed her name to Mara, meaning "bitter."

Before God used Esther, she had to risk her life to break the etiquette of the king's court to obtain favor to rescue her people from death.

Before God used Paul, first He blinded him for three days, later, He had to give him a "thorn in the flesh" to keep him from becoming prideful.

Peter denied Jesus three times. He went out and wept bitterly. In his sorrow he was convicted with a broken spirit. His brokenness led to repentance.

Even Jesus Christ's body had to be broken on the cross before the blessing of His salvation could be poured out for sinners, like you and me.

God uses broken things for His glory. In my personal experience, when I had hit rock bottom, God met me in my darkest broken place. He built me up again. I know all about brokenness. There are somethings that God can do best only when we are broken. "The LORD is close to those whose hearts are breaking; he rescues those who are humbly sorry for their sins (Psalms 34:18).

Many people in this world suffers with a broken heart, broken health, broken finances, broken limbs, broken self-esteem, broken marriages, broken relationships, broken dreams, broken friendships, and broken reputation. When your heart is broken, you feel crushed.

Brokenness is the process where God brings us to the end of ourselves and into a total trust and submission with Him. God does not want us to lean on our own understanding, but we are to lean on Him.

When we are broken, we are more willing to listen to God. In our brokenness, we become closer to God. Our brokenness brings us back into the fellowship with God. In our brokenness we become more like Christ.

God blesses brokenness. God can bless broken dreams. God can bless broken-hearts. God can bless broken lives. God can bless broken self-esteem. God can bless broken marriages. God can bless broken relationships. God can bless broken finances. God can bless our brokenness. It is through our brokenness that our light shines the brightest. God loves to shine through broken things.

SIDESHOW DISTRACTIONS

Sideshow means any diversion or distraction from the main game. A sideshow distraction is something unimportant that takes your attention away from something more important that is happening at the same time.

A distraction is anything that takes your mind off of what you are supposed to be doing. A distraction can take place in a very short period of time, or it can be something that keeps coming back again and again. Distractions prevents you from giving your full attention to something else.

Satan has a way of distracting us from God's main goal for us. Sometimes we will have the tendency to take our focus off of the prize, which is Jesus, and begin to focus on unimportant and unnecessary things and details. Things that are not an issue or shouldn't be an issue. Just plain stuff. We get caught up in the frivolous of life. Those things that would keep us from doing, seeing, and achieving what the Lord wants for us.

Satan's plan for us is to distract us, to fill our lives with substitutes for real life, to replace our affection for God and the things of God, with affection for the worldly. He knows the earthly things that we like. He knows where we are weakest, and he sets traps for us. In his system of substitution, he uses lies, idols, and deception, using physical things that he has created to pacify the human race. He stands by us, waving any number of gimmicks, toys, and any unnecessary concerns to distract us from the important things of life.

Satan uses a system of false values that God is opposed to, and have us focused on physical realities, the here and now, pleasing the relentless demands of self. He understands the human mind and heart. Charles Spurgeon says, "When Satan cannot catch us with a big sin, he will try a little one. It does not matter to him as long as he catches his fish, what bait he uses. Beware of the beginning of evil, for men who wanted to go right, have turned aside and perished amongst the dark mountains in the wide field of sin."

Some people may have their own definition of what is a distraction. Some people may not see certain things as a distraction, while others do. But distractions keeps us off focused.

The Bible constantly reminds us to stay on focus, "Watch over your heart with all diligence. For from it flow the springs of life. Put away from you a deceitful mouth. And put devious speech far from you. Let your eyes look directly ahead and let your gaze be fixed straight in front of you. Watch the path of your feet and all your ways will be established. Do not turn to the right nor to the left; turn your foot from evil" (Proverbs 4:23-27).

What does the Lord call a distraction? Anything or distraction that would take your focus off of Him and your relationship with Him. Anything or distraction that would cause you to backslide. Your relationship with God is of the highest priority. Anything that may cause you to stumble or lose focus, is a distraction.

"Let us fix our eyes on Jesus, the author and perfecter of our faith, who for the joy set before him endured the cross, scorning its shame, and sat down at the right hand of the throne of God. Consider him who endured such opposition from sinful men, so that you will not grow weary and lose heart" (Hebrews 12:2-3). We have to stay focused and always keep our eyes on Jesus. Always with Jesus on our minds and in our hearts, because when the trappings of this world catches our attention in any form or way, it is considered a sideshow distraction.

In C. S. Lewis' book, The Screwtape Letters, there are 31 letters Screwtape wrote to Wormwood, to teach him how to distract mankind. Screwtape reminds Wormwood "that mankind thinks that we put things into their minds as distractions, but our best work is done by keeping Godly things out." In his last letter in the book, letter #31, he referred to Wormwood as his poppet and pigsnie.

When we take our minds off God, we lose focus. There are dangers in losing focus. That is why the Bible tells us, "Be sober, be vigilant, because your adversary the devil, as a roaring lion, walketh about, seeking whom he may devour" (1 Peter 5:8).

There are so many types of distractions. Taking your eyes, mind, and heart off the Lord is disastrous. There is only one way to keep from being distracted. How? By keeping your eyes on the prize, Jesus. When you are focused on the Lord, He will become the guiding force of your life. Never allow a day to go by without spending time with the Lord.

If we are not careful, life will crowd Jesus out of our lives. We worry about things we have no control over. Too much worldly stuff will cause us to push Jesus away. It will take the place where God should be. We must make Jesus, the Lord of our lives. "Do not conform to the pattern of this world, but be transformed by the renewing of your mind" (Romans 12:2).

LOGOS

God's Word, the Bible, is referred to in Greek as "logos." Logos is the Greek word for, "word." It is where we get the word "logic" from. Logos is when we used cold arguments - like data, statistic, or common sense - to convince people of something, rather than trying to appeal to an audience's emotions.

"In the beginning was the Word, and the Word was with God, and the Word was God. He was with God in the beginning. Through him all things were made; without him nothing was made that has been made. In him was life, and that life was the light of men. The light shines in the darkness, but the darkness has not understood it." (John 1:1-5).

John 1:14 states, "The Word was made flesh and made his dwelling among us. We have seen his glory, the glory of the One and Only, who came from the Father, full of grace and truth."

Jesus is the Word or Logos, because "in the beginning was the Word."

Jesus is eternal and is God, and "all things were created by Him."

Jesus came and lived among us, because of His sacrificial death, "He is the Giver of Life."

Jesus is the Word of God. He is Logos. Jesus, when He came to earth was the Incarnation of God's Word, meaning what Jesus did, and what God said was the same. As the Incarnation of God's Word, Jesus' actions, and God's message are identical. Jesus' life is the Word of God. Jesus' life is the simple visual display of God's Word. Jesus is the Word of God that came down from heaven to earth, in the flesh.

Logos is the divine power of God. It is His divine command. The Bible reminds us that God's actions are His Word. His Word is powerful, because they create action. In Genesis God spoke the universe into existence, "And God said, 'Let there be light,' and there was light." God's Word controls everything. Without exception! When God said, "...Never again will I curse the ground because of man, even though every inclination of his heart is evil from childhood. And never again will I destroy all living creatures, as I have done" (Genesis 8:21). You can bet on that. What God says is what will happen, because everything is dependent on the Word of God.

Jesus is the reason why... The reason why, what? He is the reason why all things are as they are. He is the reason why everything exists. He is the reason why everything happens. The creation of all existence was made by Him. His presence among us as a human being is the most important event in the history of the universe.

God himself, in the Incarnation, chose to leave His regal throne in heaven. He got down at eye-level with man. On the cross, Jesus Himself prayed a psalm of lament, "My God, my God, why have you forsaken me?" (Matthew 27:46). In the Incarnation, He experienced what it's like to be tired, scorned, and discouraged. He knows what it is like to hurt, to be mistreated, spitted upon, and bleed. Logos is aware of ALL things including what we experience in this life, because the Word has feelings too. He is the One who wired us with our emotions.

Logos asked Isaiah some rhetorical questions in reference to who He is. He asked, "To whom will you compare me? Or who is my equal? says the Holy One. Lift your eyes and look to the heavens: Who created all these?" (Isaiah 40:25-26b). The response, "He who brings out the starry host one by one, and calls them each by name. Because of his great power and mighty strength, not one of them is missing." Then He says to Isaiah, "Do you not know? Have you not heard? The LORD is the everlasting God, The Creator of the ends of the earth. He will not grow tired or weary, and his understanding no one can fathom. He gives strength to the weary and increases the power of the weak. Even youths grow tired and weary, and young men stumble and fall; but those who hope in the LORD will renew their strength. They will soar on wings like eagles; they will run and not grow weary, they will walk and not be faint" (Isaiah 40:28-31).

The Person of God is logos. He is El Olam - the Everlasting God. He will always be the Everlasting God, without Beginning or End. He is the Creator of the ends of the earth. He created the limits, the boundaries of the earth and everything in between. God is incapable of fatigue and exhaustion - "He never grow tired." Neither does "He grow weary." He never gets tired of loving, caring, delivering, saving, healing, restoring, preserving, protecting, providing for the world. For He does it by the power of His Word.

The uncreated CREATOR, is Logos. He existed before all things.

IS ANYTHING TOO HARD FOR GOD?

"Is there anything too hard for God?" This question reveals much about God. How so? God is Sovereign. He controls all things. He is the Ultimate source of all power and authority. So when the Almighty God ask a mere mortal human a question, only God knows the answer. Whatever the question is, it is beyond the scope of any human's ability.

Take the question that the Lord asked Sarah in Genesis 18:14, "Is anything too hard for God?" The Lord appeared to Abraham while he was living in Mamre. One hot summer afternoon Abraham was sitting in his tent, when he noticed three men coming toward him. He ran to them and asked them to stay, while he refresh them with food and water. While eating, they asked Abraham, "where is Sarah, your wife?" Abraham replied, "In the tent." The Bible says, "Then the Lord said, 'Next year I will give you and Sarah a son!'" Sarah was listening and she silently laugh and said to herself, "A woman my age have a baby?" The reply was, "Is anything too hard for God?" God did as He had promised, and Sarah became pregnant and gave Abraham a baby boy in his old age, and Abraham named him, Isaac, meaning "Laughter."

When God told Moses to tell the Israelites to purify themselves because the next day He would be providing them meat to eat. This was the time that they were in the wilderness en route to the Promised Land. Moses said in Numbers 11:21-22, "There are 600,000 men alone (besides all the women and children), and yet you promise them meat for a whole month! If we butcher all our flocks and herds it won't be enough! We would have to catch every fish in the ocean to fulfill your promise!" The Lord said to Moses, "When did I become weak? Now you shall see whether my word comes true or not!" God fed the Israelites, He sent a wind that brought quail from the sea, and let them fall into the camp, all around them. God provided them with meat, bread, and water for forty years, while in the wilderness.

In Jeremiah 32, God told Jeremiah to buy a field outside of Jerusalem. The city had been under siege for a year and Jeremiah bought the land that the soldiers occupied. God promised to return His people and rebuild Jerusalem. In Jeremiah 32:17-26, Jeremiah prays to God, "O Lord God! You have made the heavens and earth by your great power; nothing is too hard for you!...And yet you say to buy the field - paying good money for it before these witnesses - even though the city will belong to our enemies." Then this message came to Jeremiah, "I am the Lord, the God of all mankind; is there anything too hard for me?"

The power of the Lord fell upon Ezekiel and carried him away to a valley full of old, dry bones that were scattered everywhere across the ground. God asked Ezekiel, "Son of dust, can these bones become people again?" Ezekiel replied, "Lord, you alone know the answer to that." The dry bones are a picture of the Jews in captivity, scattered and dead. They would be released from captivity and one day regathered in their homeland, with the Messiah. Ezekiel spoke to the dry bones and the bones responded, and just as God brought life to those dead bones, He would bring life again to the spiritually dead.

Matthew 19:16 starts with a young rich leader asking Jesus a question, "Good Master, what good thing shall I do, that I may have eternal life?" Jesus provides him with a list of things and the rich man said that he had done all those things since his youth. Then Jesus told him to sell everything he had and give it to the poor. The young man was sad, because it was his money that was keeping him from the Lord Jesus. Then Jesus made the statement, "...It is easier for a camel to go through the eye of a needle, than a rich man to enter into the kingdom of God" (v.24). What Jesus meant, many people think that they are going to be saved by who they are or what they have. You can't buy salvation. Salvation is free, through Jesus Christ. Jesus gave a response to the disciples' question, "Who then can be saved?" Jesus' response in Matthew 19:26 says, "But JESUS beheld them, and said unto them, With men this is impossible; but with God all things are possible."

When Jesus healed the demon possessed boy, the one that the disciples could not heal, in Mark 9:23, "Jesus said unto them, If thou can believe, all things are possible to him that believe." It was not a question of If Thou could do anything," because the Lord Jesus can do everything. The question was, "If thou can believe." Jesus told them that "all things are possible to him that believe."

The Word of God declares that when you believe in God, and when you put the WORD into your situation, all things become possible to him that believes. In real life, things are hard and very difficult, but not with God. Jesus is the same today as He was yesterday, and He will be the same tomorrow. God does NOT change. The things that God has said in Scripture cannot be changed, deleted, or modified, in any way. If God said not to do it, then we are NOT to do it. If God says to do it, then we ARE to do it.

John 11:40 states, "Then Jesus said, 'Did I not tell you that if you believed, you would see the glory of God?'" Jesus is still saying this to us today. Give ALL of your impossibilities to God. Place ALL of your faith in God, and watch, you will be rewarded. You will see the manifested Glory of El Shaddai, the God Almighty.

WITH JESUS ALL THINGS ARE POSSIBLE!

GOD'S SOVEREIGNTY

God is sovereign. What does this mean? God is in control! He is the Ultimate source of all power, authority, and everything that exist. He created everything that exist. To be sovereign means to have ultimate or absolute power.

God is the King of kings, Lord of lords, and the God of gods. He is without equal and limitation. He is infinite. He had no beginning and He has no ending. He is the Ruler of everything. It is recorded in the Bible, "Who is the image of the invisible God, the firstborn of every creature. For by him were all things created, that are in heaven, and that are in earth, visible and invisible, whether they be thrones, or dominions, or principalities, or powers: all things were created by him, and for him. And he is before all things, and by him all things consist" (Colossians 1:15-17).

God's sovereignty is the result of Him being Omniscient. God is all knowing. Hebrews 4:13 says, "He knows about everyone, everywhere. Everything about us is bare and wide open to the all-seeing eyes of our living God; nothing can be hidden from him to whom we must explain all that we have done.

God is Omnipotent. God is all powerful. Job 37:27 says, "The Almighty is beyond our reach and exalted in power; in his justice and great righteousness, he does not oppress." He is omnipotent in creation: "This is what the LORD says - your Redeemer, who formed you in the womb: I am the LORD, the Maker of all things, who stretches out the heavens, who spreads out the earth by myself" (Isaiah 44:24). He is omnipotent in understanding: "I made known the end from the beginning, from ancient times, what is still to come. I say, 'My purpose will stand, and I will do all that I please.' From the east I summon a bird of prey; from a far-off land, a man to fulfill my purpose. What I have said, that I will bring about; what I have planned, that I will do" (Isaiah 46:10-11).

God is Omnipresent. God is present everywhere at all times with no exceptions. There is no place you can hide from God, and no where that you can be that God is not there. "Can a man hide himself in secret places so that I cannot see him? declares the Lord. Do I not fill heaven and earth? declares the Lord?" (Jeremiah 23:24). There is no place you can be that God is not also there, and aware of. God fills both heaven and earth, so there is nowhere that humans can go that God is not already there, before they get there. David says, "Where shall I go from your Spirit? Or where shall I flee from your presence? If I ascend to heaven, you are there! If I make my bed in Sheol, you are there! If I take the wings of the morning and dwell in the uttermost parts of the sea, even there your hand shall lead me, and your right hand shall hold me" (Psalm 139:7-10)

The Bible describes God as all-powerful, all-knowing, outside of time, and responsible for the creation of everything. Nothing in this universe can happen without God's permission. God knows what will happen today, tomorrow, and 100 years from now, and He has a plan for each and everyday. He is aware of every second, minute, and hour. He knows the details of our days. God knows our thoughts. God knows the paths of our lives and every direction of our lives. God knows the words we will say before the thoughts are formed in our mind. God is always with us, regardless of what or how we feel. He is there in our sorrow, disappointment, trouble, and pain. He is there in our joy and laughter too. He is always there when no one else is.

God's sovereignty means that anything that comes into your life, God either decreed it or allowed it. Whatever God has allowed to enter your life, you must be willing to trust Him, because He can work it out for your good. "In him we have obtained an inheritance, having been predestined according to the purpose of him who works all things according to the counsel of his will" (Ephesians 1:11). This means, every single event that occurs in your life and in this world, is predestined by God. In regards to tragedies and evil, God cannot be blamed. He either allows it for His purpose, or He overcomes it for His purpose.

JUST UNIQUELY YOU

God created each of us to be special and unique. No two people are created exactly alike. We all have our own individual personalities, dreams, talents, gifts, ideas, thoughts, and behavior.

Accepting who we are, our individuality, sometimes becomes a lifetime lesson. Sometimes, we will compare ourselves to others. When you compare yourself to someone else, you are insulting God. God is the Creator of all things, and that includes you. When you are unhappy with how God has made you, you are telling God that you are married and His masterpiece isn't good enough. What an insult! God doesn't do flaws nor are you a mistake. You are who you are supposed to be, because that is how God wants you to be. We are all different from each other. We look different. We act different. We think different.

When you compare yourself to someone else, this is a recipe for unhappiness. Comparison is one of the enemy's schemes. The enemy wants you to self-sabotage so you can self-destruct. When you start comparing yourself to others, you are lifting the other person up and bringing yourself down. There is one thing that you are excellent at, and that is being you. No one can do you, better than you.

You are uniquely you. God made you to be who you are. God made you to look the way you look, even your walk is uniquely you. God is the Potter and we are the clay. He made us all perfect in His image and we all have our own uniqueness. We were made for a purpose. God has a plan for each of us and we are all a member of the body of Christ. We are God's masterpiece. God wants you to see how special and uniquely He created you.

The Bible says:

"It is God himself who has made us what we are and given us new lives from Christ Jesus; and long ages ago he planned that we should spend these lives in helping others" (Ephesians 2:10).

So God created man in his own image, in the image of God he created him; male and female he created them" (Genesis 1:27).

"You alone created my inner being. You knitted me together inside my mother. I will give thanks to you because I have been so amazingly and miraculously made. Your works are miraculous, and my soul is fully aware of this" (Psalm 139:13-14).

Showers of Blessings

"But God, being rich in mercy, because of the great love with which he loved us, even when we were dead in our trespasses, made us alive together with Christ -- by grace you have been saved -- and raised us up with him and seated us with him in the heavenly places in Christ Jesus, so that in the coming ages he might show the immeasurable riches of his grace in kindness toward us in Christ Jesus. For by grace you have been saved through faith. And this is not your own doing; it is the gift of God" (Ephesians 2:4-9).

"You made me; you created me. Now give me the sense to follow your commands. May all who fear you find in me a cause for joy, for I have put my hope in your word" (Psalm 119:73-74).

"Bring my sons from afar and my daughters from the ends of the earth -- everyone who is called by my name, whom I created for my glory, whom I formed and made" (Isaiah 43:6-7).

For he chose us in him before the creation of the world to be holy and blameless in his sight" (Ephesians 1:4).

"Have you forgotten that your body is not the sacred temple of the Spirit of Holiness, who lives in you? You don't belong to yourself any longer, for the gift of God, the Holy Spirit, lives inside your sanctuary. You were God's expensive purchase, paid for with tears of blood, so by all means, then, use your body to bring glory to God!" (1 Corinthians 6:19-20).

"You were there while I was being formed in utter seclusion! You saw me before I was born and scheduled each day of my life before I began to breathe. Every day was recorded in your Book!" (Psalm 139:15-16).

"See what great love the Father has lavished on us, that we should be called children of God! And that is what we are!" (1 John 3:1a).

"For I know the plans I have for you, declares the Lord, plans for welfare and not for evil, to give you a future and a hope. Then you will call upon me and come and pray to me, and I will hear you. You will seek me and find me, when you seek me with all your heart" (Jeremiah 29:11-13).

"I will instruct you and teach you in the way you should go; I will counsel you with my loving eye on you" (Psalm 32:8).

"But you are a chosen people, a royal priesthood, a holy nation, God's special possession, that you may declare the praises of him who called you out of darkness into his wonderful light" (1 Peter 2:9).

God wants you to accept who you are and place your focus on Him. He wants you to improve your relationship with Him. Your relationship with Jesus is most important. God loves you and He has shown His love for you through an unique manner, when He created you. He created you and He will always be there to guide you on the path He has chosen for you. His presence in your life keeps you on His chosen path. He wants us to love Him, love ourselves, and to love others. He wants us to be Christ-like, ever-growing and ever-learning. God made you to be just uniquely you.

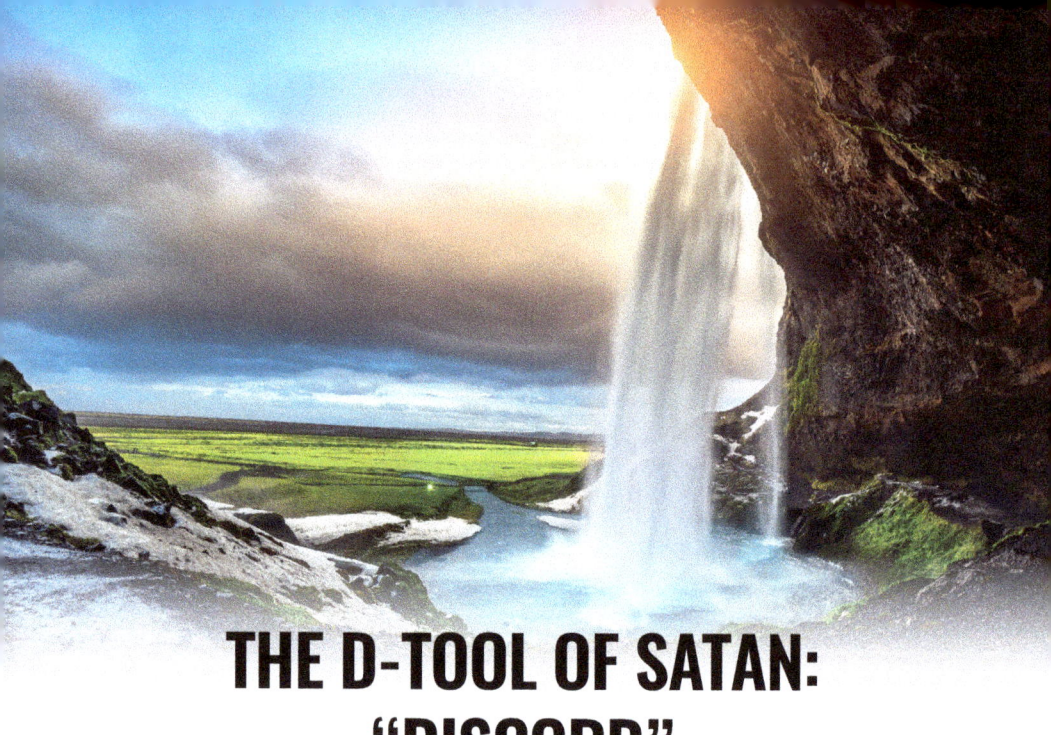

THE D-TOOL OF SATAN: "DISCORD"

Sowing discord is one of the most heinous sins in the Bible. It is a wicked sin fathered by pride and it was found in Lucifer, when he was in heaven. He sowed discord, to a third of God's Holy angels, who was persuaded to disobey God. Sowing discord is done, usually in secret, through sneakiness, gossip, lies, and deception. The father and author of discord is Satan. All sowers of discord are those who breathes lies and deceit. Sowers of discord will usually start off small, like a trail of water, then it flows to other places, causing flooding everywhere, causing sometimes, irreparable damage in hearts and minds.

To sow discord, is doing things to cause distrust among one another, which can result into arguments, fights, and death. People can pass vicious rumors, not knowing that they are unintentionally sowing discord. Spreading rumors is one of the many ways of sowing discord. The Bible says, "Whoever covers an offense seeks love, but he who repeats a matter separates close friends" (Proverbs 17:9).

Sowing discord is an abomination and is totally detestable in the eyes of the Lord. "There are six things that the Lord hates, seven that are an abomination to him: haughty eyes, a lying tongue, and hands that shed innocent blood, a heart that devises wicked plans, feet that make haste to run to evil, a false witness who breathes out lies, and one who sows discord among the brothers" (Proverbs 6:16-19). God hates discord and denounce those who sows strife. "A perverse man sow's strife, and a whisperer separates the best of friends" (Proverbs 16:28).

God hates discord! Some people are far to ready to stir up strife, quarrels, fights, either for money, power, revenge, control, envy, or for their own glory and honor, or it could be for a combination of these reasons. The Bible says, "Let me describe for you a worthless and a wicked man; first, he is a constant liar; he signals his true intentions to his friends with eyes and feet and fingers. He is always thinking up new schemes to swindle people. He stirs up trouble everywhere" (Proverbs 6:12-14). This is the type of person that does something for their own gratification, satisfying their own evil desires. They deceive people to please themselves. They are telling lies and deceiving people and causing division. They are self-gratifying, sowing the seeds of bitterness, anger, distrust, and hatred into the ground of other people's hearts. These actions comes from the spirit of the deceiver, the devil. They are "the works of the flesh." "Now the deeds of the flesh are evident, which are: immorality, impurity, sensuality, idolatry, sorcery, enmities, strife, jealousy, outbursts of anger, disputes, dissensions, factions, envying, drunkenness, carousing, and things like these, of which I forewarn you, just as I have forewarned you, that those who practice such things will not inherit the kingdom of God" (Galatians 5:20-21).

To sow, means to plant seeds. The one who sows seeds of discord, carefully chooses the circumstance and the victim or victims. The intent is to deliberately produce discord to hurt or discredit that person, in some way or another. The sower of the discord, has a nasty, corrupt, evil spirit that produces a harvest of discord. What kind of seeds produce a harvest of discord? The seed of pride, selfishness, back-biting, gossip, bitterness, jealousy, and the likes.

Sowers of discord, are driven to serve their own evil and dark interests. They exploit the emotions and passions of others, because they receive pleasure from causing conflicts and harm. They are playing into the hands of the dark spiritual forces.

God hates discord and He hates those who sow discord. As children of God, we must do everything to avoid sowing discord, intentionally or unintentionally. Remember, every idle word we speak will come under judgment. "You brood of snakes! How could evil men like you speak what is good and right? For a man's heart determines his speech. A good man's speech reveals the rich treasures within him. An evil-hearted man is filled with venom, and his speech reveals it. And I tell you this, that you must give account on Judgment Day for every idle word you speak. Your words now reflect your fate: either you will be justified by them or you will be condemned" (Matthew 12:34-37).

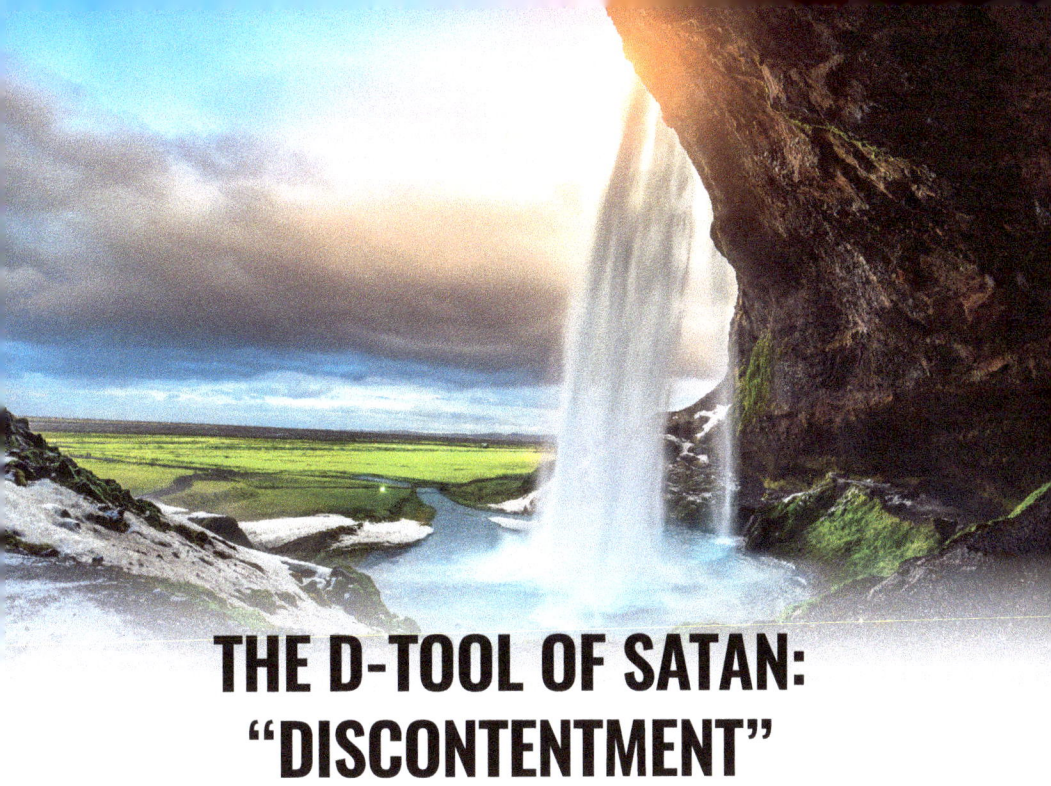

THE D-TOOL OF SATAN: "DISCONTENTMENT"

We are at war! Satan hates us, and he wants to destroy us. The enemy has many tricks up his sleeves. He is very good at what he does. He loves to play mind games with us and one such game is planting seeds of discontentment. He will plant them all along our pathway of life. Seeds of dissatisfaction, displeasure, disappointment, depression, disillusion, frustration, resentment, bitterness, misery, sadness, and unhappiness.

Satan wants you to feel stuck in your life. He wants you struggling with an overall feeling of unhappiness. The enemy wants you to focus on what you do not have. He wants you to always be angry and never at peace. He wants you frustrated and never satisfied. Discontentment comes from the heart. You start thinking over and over again, that you don't deserve the hand that you were dealt. You start thinking, consistently, I deserve better and I deserve to get better. You may even have the nerves to blame God for your current situation.

If you analyze discontentment, you will discover many reasons that causes discontentment. There is a constant craving for something that we don't have. Adam and Eve craved for the forbidden fruit. David craved for someone else's wife. There are many examples in the Bible about discontentment. Since the beginning of time, starting with Eve, we have been an unhappy group of people. After Eden, we have never fully been satisfied. If we are young, we want to be older. If we are old, we wish we were younger. If it is small, we want it bigger. If it is new, we want something newer. If we are skinny, we want to gain weight. If we are overweight we want to be skinny.

If you have an apartment, you want a condo. If you have a condo, you want a house. Or a new house. Or a bigger house. If you have a job, you want a better job, a bigger job, a closer job, with a bigger office, a better boss, better benefits, bigger and better opportunities. We always want what we do not have, because we think that the other thing is better for us, just because we do not have it.

Discontentment, can and will, manifest into pride. What is pride? Pride is sin. The sin of pride is an excessive preoccupation with self and one's own importance, achievements, status, or possessions. This sin is considered rebellion against God. Pride is called "the cancer of the soul."

Pride becomes sinful when it becomes excessively, self-focused and self-elevating. The Biblical sin of pride refers to a high or an exalted attitude. It is the opposite of humility. The Bible has many verses about pride: "When pride comes, then comes disgrace, but with humility comes wisdom" (Proverbs 11:2). Proverbs 8:13 says, "To fear the LORD is to hate evil; I hate pride and arrogance, evil behavior and perverse speech." James 4:6-7 says, "But he gives more and more strength to stand against all such evil longings. As the Scripture says, God gives strength to the humble, but sets himself against the proud and haughty. So give yourself humbly to God, Resist the devil and he will flee from you."

I once had a co-worker who drove me crazy, because she was always putting herself on a pedestal. Each and everyday she would come into my office ranting about what she deserved. Her complaints were taller than herself. She deserved a larger salary. She deserved a higher position. She would make the comment, "Look at me! Don't I look like I deserve more than what I have?" I was never aware that what you looked like made you more favorable or important than someone else. Now, she was the epitome of a walking definition of "pride."

Pride goes before destruction. Satan knows all about "pride." Satan fell from heaven. Why did he fall from heaven? He fell from heaven because of pride, he was wrapped in discontentment. He desired to be God, not to be a servant of God. Wait a minute, Satan did not really fall from heaven, he was pushed out. No! He was really, kicked-out of heaven. The devil is the proudest creature and the most discontented one, and he wants you to feel the same way as he does.

Pride leaves you to think that you deserve better than what God has given you, instead of thinking that you have everything you need. God is such a wonderful and awesome God. He doesn't give us what we really deserve. God loves us so much, instead of us spending eternity in hell, with fire and brimstone, He gave us His Son, and not what we deserved.

Thanks to God, we have a Savior who forgives us of our sins, who can help us grow in contentment. For Jesus has told us, "to be content with what we have." "Be content with such things you have" means, that you should put your trust and confidence in God, knowing that He is the Giver of all good things and He uses even the hard times to show us that He is faithful.

God wants us to, seek first His kingdom and His righteousness, "...for your heavenly Father knoweth that ye have need of all these things. But seek ye the kingdom of God, and his righteousness; and all these things shall be added unto you" (Matthew 6:32-33). God is the secret to contentment. Discontentment is a sin!

THE D-TOOL OF SATAN: "DISCOURAGEMENT"

"For our struggle is not against flesh and blood, but against the rulers, against the authorities, against the powers of this dark world and against the spiritual forces of evil in the heavenly realms" (Ephesians 6:22).

If the spiritual veil was lifted, we would be completely overwhelmed, disturbed, and shocked about what our eyes would behold. There is a spiritual war going on. It is a fight-to-the death battle, between good and evil. We know that the battle has already been won, but that doesn't mean that evil is dead. Absolutely not! Evil is all around us and evil wants to conquer as many of God's children as it can.

The devil has many schemes, tricks, and weapons that are used to trip us up and set us back. One such weapon is DISCOURAGEMENT.

The Apostle Paul faced many and great difficulties in his ministry. The Book of 2 Corinthians, chapter four is the preeminent chapter on Paul overcoming discouragement. "We are troubled on every side, yet not distressed; we are perplexed, but not in despair; Persecuted, but not forsaken; cast down, but not destroyed; always bearing about in the body the dying of the Lord Jesus, that the life also of Jesus might be made manifest in our body" (vv. 8-10).

The seeds of discouragement are planted all throughout the Bible, from the Old Testament to the New Testament. And today, the enemy is still sowing seeds of discouragement throughout the lives of everyone of God's children.

My late husband shared an old story that goes like this. The devil was having a garage sale, putting on a display of some of his best wares. Demons came from all around to see what they could purchase to improve their shameful skill.

The story goes on to say that the goods were useful, but pricey, until the demons noticed that there in the corner was an old worn and tattered box priced far above all the other evil tools of the trade. Finally, a demon worked up the courage to ask the devil why was that old box so expensive and the devil said, "Why that is the tool that I have used most often and with the greatest amount of success! This tool is called, discouragement." All the demons nodded in agreement.

The enemy will plant seeds of discouragement in your walk with God. Oh, yes! He wants to creep in your heart and plant that crippling seed to get you to alter your walk of faith. He wants you to question God and His goodness.

I know you have heard the old saying, "Bad things happen to good people." It's true, but we shouldn't be surprised when it happens. The enemy will plant seeds of tribulation in your path through sickness, joblessness, and all kinds of pestilence. He will try to steal your joy. He will bring chaos in your home. He will ruin an excellent relationship with your spouse, friends, relatives, even in your church. He will try to even shame you. He will do ANYTHING to overwhelm you and to bring you down emotionally.

Discouragement is the cleverish tool that Satan has in his entire arsenal. Because discouragement is his most effective tool. Discouragement is a dangerous state of mind. It leaves you open to assault. The devil sometimes use the ones that we really love or care about to discourage us. He will use those who we love and respect, to be insensitive to us, especially with words that wounds. He will use what we care about to break us down.

The enemy is so clever, because he can plant seeds of discouragement from our own way of thinking, through misinterpretation or misunderstanding. Just because it may seem difficult, doesn't mean that it is bad. When things don't turn out the way we hoped for, we become discouraged, telling ourselves that we have failed or the "woe is me" thought have us sprouting seedlings of discouragement.

Seeds of discouragement are also planted when our long awaited prayer has not been answered. This time of silence from God, the enemy will use against us. He will use God's silence as a source of discouragement. He will try to make you think that God's silence in your life is a result of your lack of love for God or God's lack of love for you. The enemy wants you to doubt your relationship with God and doubt His love for you.

The only way to fight discouragement is to trust God. God loves us, therefore, we must do our part in loving and trusting Him. We must rest in the assurance, that no matter what is happening in our lives, He will always be with us, because He will never leave us nor forsake us. Dr. Charles Stanley said, "Discouragement is a choice. You don't have to remain discouraged no matter what is going on in your life."

Discouragement is a personal attack on us and we have to fight against it. Some people are confronted with it more than others. Psalm 55:22 says, "Cast your burden on the LORD, and He shall sustain you; He shall never permit the righteous to be moved." We are also reminded, "Do not fret or have any anxiety about anything, but in every circumstance and in everything, by prayer and petition (definite requests), with thanksgiving, continue to make your wants known to God. And God's peace [shall be yours, that tranquil state of a soul assured of its salvation through Christ, and so fearing nothing from God and being content with its earthly lot of whatever sort that is, that peace] which transcends all understanding shall garrison and mount guard over your hearts and minds in Christ Jesus" (Philippians 4:6-7). God is always at work in our lives and many times we can't see it, but nevertheless, He is at work for us, working it out for our good.

THE D-TOOL OF SATAN: "DOUBT"

Satan has many tricks up his sleeves and he is the author of lies. He is as slick as they come and he is an evil master controller. He is very good at what he does. He was once a heavenly angel. His name was Lucifer, which means "star of the morning." He held a high ranking position in the heavenly host. He was described as an exceedingly beautiful angel with great wisdom. He was given a position of great power and influence. He was called "the guardian cherub." The Bible says, "You were the perfection of wisdom and beauty. You were in Eden, the garden of God; your clothing was bejeweled with every precious stone -- ruby, topaz, diamond, chrysolite, onyx, jasper, sapphire, carbuncle, and emerald -- all in beautiful settings of finest gold. They were given to you on the day you were created. I appointed you to be the anointed Guardian Angel. You had access to the holy mountain of God. You walked among the stones of fire. You were perfect in all you did from the day you were created until that time when wrong was found in you. Your great wealth filled you with internal turmoil and you sinned. Therefore, I cast you out of the mountain of God like a common sinner. I destroyed you, O Guardian Angel, from the midst of the stones of fire. Your heart was filled with pride because of all your beauty; you corrupted your wisdom for the sake of your splendor. Therefore I have cast you down to the ground and exposed you helpless before the curious gaze of kings" (Ezekiel 28:12-17).

Lucifer (the star of the morning) became Satan (the accuser) when he was kicked out of heaven. When he was kicked out, he was not kicked out alone. Scripture tells us that one-third of the angels in heaven was kicked out with him. They are the fallen angels or demons that wreak havoc on God's people. They are powerful spirit beings with demonic powers to help Satan accomplished his purpose. What is his purpose? Jesus says that the enemy comes to "steal, kill, and destroy" (John 10:10).

Every day of our lives, we are in the combat zone. We are in a spiritual warfare. Because we are fighting spiritual beings, they will plant all types of negative thoughts in our mind. There are many weapons the devil will use against those who belong to Jesus. He is not worried about those who belong to him, because he knows that a house divided cannot stand. His number one job is to attack Jesus' flock.

There are many weapons he uses against us today. I am going to discuss the "D-tool of doubt." This weapon has been used throughout the ages. The very first question in the Bible came from Satan when he tempted Eve in the garden, he asked her a question, "Did God really say, 'You must not eat from any tree in the garden'?" (Genesis 3:1). He had only one purpose, to sow the seed of doubt in her mind. He wanted Adam and Eve to doubt what God had told them, and it worked. That is why Jesus reminds us that the devil is "the father of lies." Doubt is a poisonous seed, planted by our enemy. Once the seed is planted in someone's head and heart, it takes root. Then the enemy cultivates this poisonous seed, called doubt. Then we fester on it, and when we fester on it, we fertilize it.

Doubt is a very powerful tool that Satan uses on us. One of Jesus' disciples carried the baggage of doubt, like a noose tied around his neck. In John 20, the disciples had gathered together to share the joy of seeing the risen Christ, but there was one disciple who was not there, Thomas. Thomas had not seen Jesus since His death, but the others had seen Him. Thomas said, "Unless I see the nail marks in his hand and put my finger where the nails were, and put my hand into his side, I will not believe." The Bible warns us about doubt, "But when you ask, you must believe and not doubt, because the one who doubts is like a wave of the sea, blown and tossed by the wind" (James 1:6). Only God can help you fight against the trials and temptations that Satan will bring your way.

Satan even tempted Jesus while in the wilderness over two thousand years ago. To this day, nothing has changed about him. Satan is still telling lies of deception as he seeks to keep mankind from listening to the voice of God. He attacks us to make us doubt the voice of Jesus. He tells us creative half-truths, to make us doubt God's promises, causing us to think wrongly about God. Remember, half-truths are still, lies.

Doubt is one of Satan's ways to turn people away from God. He will even have you to doubt your faith. Some of the most faithful Christians struggle with doubt sometimes. Just like the man who asked Jesus to heal his son in Mark 9, Jesus told him, "all things are possible for one who believes." Then the father cried, "I do believe; help me overcome my unbelief!" (vv. 23-24).

Doubt can be combated by faith and trust, because faith and trust goes hand in hand. The enemy throws a shadow over our faith and trust, by using doubt. God can help us through it all. Faith is trusting God even when we just don't understand what's going on. Even when nothing makes absolutely no sense. Faith is relying on what we do know (who is God), to get us by, when we are faced with something that we do not understand.

www.ingramcontent.com/pod-product-compliance
Lightning Source LLC
Chambersburg PA
CBHW040802150426
42811CB00056B/1132